Korean Youth Transitions:
Korean Youth Bearing the Future of Korean Community in the United States

Hermit Kingdom Sources in Korean-American Studies (No. 1)
Series Editor:
Professor Onyoo Elizabeth Kim, Ph.D., JD
Han-Dong University Law School

KOREAN YOUTH TRANSITIONS:

Korean Youth Bearing the Future of Korean Community in the United States

Edited by
Francis Won

The Hermit Kingdom Press
Highland Park * Seoul * Bangalore * Cebu

Korean Youth Transitions:
Korean Youth Bearing the Future of Korean
Community in the United States
(Hermit Kingdom Sources in Korean-American Studies, 1)

Copyright ©2009 The Hermit Kingdom Press

Hardcover ISBN13: 978-1-59689-088-6
Paperback ISBN13: 978-1-59689-099-2

Write To Address:
The Hermit Kingdom Press
P. O. Box 1226
Highland Park, NJ 08904-1226
The United States of America

Library of Congress Cataloging-in-Publication Data

Korean youth transitions : Korean youth bearing the future of Korean community in the United States / edited by Francis Won. -- 1st ed.
    p. cm.
 ISBN 978-1-59689-088-6 (hardcover : alk. paper) -- ISBN 978-1-59689-099-2 (pbk. : alk. paper)
 1. Korean American teenagers--Biography 2. Korean American teenagers--Ethnic identity. 3. Koreans--United States--Biography. 4. Koreans--United States--Ethnic identity. 5. High school students--United States--Biography. 6. Immigrants--United States--Biography. 7. United States--Emigration and immigration. 8. Korea--Emigration and immigration. I. Won, Francis.
 E184.K6K64 2009
 305.2350895'70973--dc22

                          2009044836

Contents

FORWARD

I am pleased to celebrate the publication of this important book, which is monumentally important for Korean Studies at the university level as well as for understanding Koreans at the popular level.

I would like to commend particularly Won-Hyuk (Peter) Choi for his achievement and for his autobiography in this important book. I have known him for years through my close relationship with his father and family and watched him grow from a cheerful and playful boy to a charming young man.

As a child, he was always happy and cordial. More recently, as an ambitious high school student, he asked for my helped in finding a volunteer position at one of our engineering labs at Ehwa Women's University during summer of 2009.

Ehwa Women's University is the best all-female university in South Korea, with leading researchers and professors in every field. Our university sends elite students in engineering and other fields to Ph.D. programs at MIT, CalTech, Stanford, Harvard, Oxford, Cambridge, Paris (Sorbonne), Heidelberg, Munich, Berlin, Moscow State, and McGill, to name a few of the elite universities around the world which benefit from our students' participation.

From the start, I was particularly impressed with Won-Hyuk's initiative to seek a position at a women's university, which I thought most boys would shy away from. But this just illustrates Won-Hyuk's open mind and desire to learn from the best engineers in Korea. Once he started the volunteer research work, he immediately demonstrated his enthusiasm and quickly helped out with labor intensive work of the lab. In addition, he showed his intellectual curiosity through attentive observation and assistance. Throughout the summer, he was punctual and dependable. He contributed to the team with his cheerful demeanor and sense of responsibility.

I congratulate Won-Hyuk and other authors for publishing their autobiographies in this important book. It is because of future leaders as the authors in this book that South Korea is certain to remain a global leader in consumer electronics, nanotechnology, and industrial design engineering.

I personally look forward to the future success of every one of the authors in this important book. Maybe Won-Hyuk and others may come back to their home country of South Korea and serve as professors of leading Korean universities, such as our university, Ehwa Women's University.

Bae-Yong Lee
President, Ehwa Women's University, South Korea
President, Korean Universities Academic Association

PREFACE

I would like to commend Francis Won for editing this wonderful and historically significant book, which is a valuable gem for Korean people around the world. I give my support for this publishing of our stories.

I particularly would like to commend Francis for his autobiography. In his writing, Francis offers a unique perspective that reflects not only the history of his personal journey, but also that of his family and his native country that unveils political, social, and religious transformations, which occurred in the past century. It is a story of hope and courage in the midst of changes and chances in life told in an honest and unpretentious way that invites the readers to experience grace and openness that underlines the story.

With many absorbing and memorable tales, it speaks to the heart of humanity that strives to see beyond one's challenges and circumstances in life and find hope with faith. We get a glimpse of a family that seeks to live out their faith in various situations and challenges and of a young man's journey of finding his place and identity that embraces the essence of the family's tradition and legacy.

I highly recommend this book and hope that this story along with other stories in this monumentally important book of Korean youth voices would inspire many to find hope and courage in their struggles in life.

Peace,

Rev. Joseph S. Pae
Canon Pastor
Cathedral of the Incarnation
50 Cathedral Avenue
Garden City, New York 11530
(516) 746-2955

The History of the Korean Anglican (Episcopalian) Church

Rev. Ho Gil Won
Rector, Saint Peter's Korean Episcopalian Church

The Korean Anglican Church was founded by Bishop Charles John Corfe on November 1, 1889. It was Bishop Corfe's first mission from the Archbishop of Canterbury after his consecration. After gathering supporters for the mission, he set sail and arrived at Incheon harbor on September 29, 1890, and quickly began to spread the gospel in the region.

To help spread the gospel faster; Bishop Corfe founded several academic schools, hospitals, and orphanages in the area with the purpose of educating the people. In order to better understand Korean culture, Bishop Corfe had the buildings as well as the churches built in the Korean style of architecture. Most of the buildings built are still around to this day.

Beginning in 1914 mission work was actively carried out in the northern part of the peninsula such as Pyongan and Hwanghae Provinces. To train the local clergy, St. Michael's Seminary, the institution now known as Sung Kong Hoe University, was established in 1923, followed by the Society of the Holy Cross (convent) in 1925. In 1926 the cathedral Church of St. Mary the Virgin and St. Nicholas, located in downtown Seoul, was constructed. The church is well renowned for its unique Romanesque architecture, as it is the only one built in this style in Asia, as well as its mosaic murals.

The first Korean bishop, Cheon Hwan Lee, was ordained twenty years after the liberation of Korea from Japan in 1965. After the consecration of Bishop Lee, the Korean Diocese of the Anglican Church was separated into the Seoul Diocese and the Daejeon Diocese. In 1974 the Daejeon Diocese was separated into the current Daejeon Diocese and the Pusan Diocese.

On its centennial anniversary on September 29, 1990, the Anglican Church of Korea decided to continue proclaiming the message of life to the people and showed its support for the peaceful reunification of Korea under the theme "Jesus Christ, Life of the Nation".

The Provincial Constitution of the Anglican Church of Korea was declared on September 29, 1992 and the first Korean primate was inducted on April 16, 1993. The Church finally became an independent national church with commitment to sharing the gospel with the people and rededicating itself to the Lord's will.

Currently more than 100 churches are in service nationwide, with approximately 50, 000 believers and missionaries being educated through programs such as Na Num Ui Jip (House of Sharing) Mission. The House of Shalom Ministry assists immigrant workers in finding jobs as well as protecting them from racial discrimination in their works.

To my son Francis,

It seems like it was only yesterday when I walked you to kindergarten; to think that you would be leaving our side to go off to a foreign place to live with strangers creates a heavy burden in my heart. I suppose that is how most parents would feel when their child leaves for college.

I remember when you were a child, you loved to read. I would rarely see you without a book in your hand, and if you found a book that you truly loved, you would read it all the way into the night.

Thinking back on when you were a child makes my heart heavy, as this is similar to the day you entered elementary school in Canada despite the fact you hardly spoke English.

Every time I remember the day when a boy at your school ridiculed you and spat on you, and me not being able help you because I couldn't speak English fluently; it brings tears to my eyes, and I pray that that sort of incident never happen to you again.

Yet, despite this sort of hardship, you managed to live out your life without any problems, and I thank God for that. I am thankful that although you are leaving our side, at least you are leaving this book to us as a reminder.

I continue to pray that God will offer you protection for the rest of your life, as well as helping you live out your dreams.

Live a healthy and eventful life.

Your father,

Rev. Ho Gil Won
Rector
Saint Peter's Korean Episcopal Church
335 79th Street, North Bergen, New Jersey 07047
201-869-6331

IN MY LIFE

John Lee

In the early hours of this urban neighborhood, when God's eye strikes the Earth and that intangible holy rain illuminates the dark awakened streets, soaking the trees' leaves, and dripping warm phantom nectar onto the cold cement which holds traces of the chilly autumn night from yesterday, blue collar workers awaken from drunken slumber or blissful escape from the hardships of cleaning floors, washing feet, and long nights at the cashier. Children are rudely awakened from their beds, hurried by their mothers to the shower, then breakfast, and finally to school. The public school kids walk melancholically to the tall, grey, foreboding prison people call the "highway outta'

here," or basically school. The Catholic school kids no different from kids going to public school, except wearing green blazers and small tweedy suits, lumber on to the small red open doors of the red brick building with big letters on the top that says, "St. Francis of Assisi Catholic School." To parents those words mean a safer place for their kids instead of the dirty and delinquent filled public school. To the kids who go there the words mean strict nuns, boring lectures, and time that would be better spent elsewhere. While the children go off on their dramatic funeral march to school, the parents get ready for work, another hard day of labor for them of course; the only redemption that the day offers them is the 2 hours spent in front of the TV after coming from work and getting knocked out from booze or the Atlas shaking exhaustion.

When school's all done however, the kids run off, blazing in a hundred different directions like fireworks, going from here to there, the boiling aching desire of fun being repressed all day now exploding like a volcano. The two most prominent places they could go would be the park or the zoo, which is close by. The park, like any other park, holds the basic equipment necessary for it to be labeled a park, swings, play sets, etc. While it is basic, to the kids, it is the hole down into Alice's wonderland, a place where they can play their games and act different characters that are only limited by their imagination. The zoo on the other hand offers a different kind of escape. The tunnel leading to the entrance of the zoo is painted with dozens of water color and spray painted pictures of animals from all over the world. The zoo itself holds the real life counterparts of these animals, their real visceral skin and temperament fascinate the young and the old alike, from the staring monkeys, to the lazy lions, and then to the flittering birds.

After the afternoon's excitement however, the kid's return home and the parents return from work. The night comes down like a black curtain, and any comfort from the sun is forcefully shaved off like bushy hair on a chin. The echoes of warmth forcing up Goosebumps on people's skin force them to enter the warm comfort of home. After all is said and done the children go about the rest of the night peacefully or are punished by their parents for various troubles of the day. The parents on the other hand, apart from playing enforcers, go about paying taxes, bills, all the responsibilities of adults, but when it all becomes too much they escape into the recesses of the past, into happier times, perhaps young love or prospects of wild dreams, only to be rudely awakened by the newborn's crying screams. The pen drops, bills and papers, stowed away, and then off to bed, double and together if the marriage is going well, or single and separate if a rift disturbs the happy marriage image like cracks on a window screen. And then the day is finally done, people shut off their lights, and after giving a prayer to the Lord, shut down their conscious minds, and open up their subconscious hearts where they, along with everyone in this side of the world, fly together in the field of dreams.

This is my hometown, Morris Park, The Bronx. This is where I was born and grew up. This is where it all started.

I was born in December 19, 1992, in a hospital in the Bronx. My family was Catholic so I was named after

Saint John, a holy man who apparently died on the same day I was born. I never really cared about who Saint John really was because John was such a generic name and the fact the I was named after a saint always came as a bit of an irony to me because of the way I acted as a child and perhaps still today (which you might guess is not so polite and courteous. Think of me as a young Marlon Brando or at the very least a rough cut out of a mentally challenged clown). I don't remember much of my very early days, but the earliest memory I have is during the time my family took a long road trip throughout America. We were on this long highway from here to nowhere, where I just saw stretches of barren land going to the horizon and beyond. The sky was pure white, the road was gravelly and rough, and there was just this long, stretching highway in front of us leading us to some destination, a place I never really remembered. The goal of that journey across that road I never will remember, but the journey to it will always be in my mind, that emptiness, that vastness, and my family, all four of us, me, my sister, my dad, and my mom, we were like the only people in the world during that space of time, leading to nowhere. I've always felt like my life until now has always been like that time. Just me alone, on this lonely road, going somewhere that I can't figure out, where the sights around me give me no clues or signs of any previous human beings having been there already and the empty sky, that blank sheet of white, a mirror of everything that has never happened to me in my life, just alone, with nowhere to go, on a lost highway. But enough of that; more on the road trip.

We visited various places but one prominent location comes to mind. It was this hotel, I don't remember the name, but a very special moment occurred here. It was the time where I nearly drowned, died, and had a very special experience which I could only describe as very, very strange and mystic. The hotel had this pool and my family and I were there having a good time. I couldn't swim so I swam in the tiny kiddy pool on the side that was like 2 feet high. I quickly grew bored of this so I got out of the kiddy pool and walked along the side of the huge pool. I remember being rather awed by the huge depth of the pool. Right now I probably would just think of it as being like any other pool, but back then I was just a tiny human being and everything looked colossal in my eyes and the pool was no different. I was just minding my own business, walking back and forth the poolside like a pendulum, when all of a sudden my feet slipped and I fell with a resounding splash into the pool. I can't really describe the feeling I felt during that time because everything was happening at once, water was filling up my lungs, I was losing consciousness fast, and my arms were flailing sluggishly in the depths of that liquid hell. Fear, terror, remorse, none of that, just this single basic instinct that screamed in my mind: Get Out. But my body couldn't hold out, and I just lost consciousness.

Here's where the weird part starts. Just moments before I completely blacked out all of a sudden, I had this strange vision. I was still in the water but I saw this boy trying to move his arms helplessly in the water, and he kept falling and falling into the depths of the pool, bubbles bursting to the surface like the seconds of life he had left to live. I realized that the boy was me and that I was viewing myself from the outside, from a 3rd person perspective. It was like the strings that tethered me to life were being cut one by one and my spirit just lingered outside my body for a moment before floating away into the abyss. After this strange moment I remember waking up suddenly in someone's arms. It was the lifeguard's and I was coughing up water like a hydrant. He said a few things like, "he should get some rest," and stuff like that and after staying conscious for a few seconds I fell unconscious again. Only, the next time, I woke up in the comfort of a warm bed. That was one of the first experiences of my life that I remember. A great start isn't it?

If I had to describe my life in Morris Park, I would probably have to say it was the happiest time of my life, a time where I felt I had people, a time where I felt in place, a place where I belonged, but it was also the beginning of everything going wrong. My family was a group of four, including me, my sister Christina, my mom Mi Sook Kim, and my dad Doo Jin Lee. My sister was a normal teenage girl, interested in girls' magazines, the Spice Girls, extremely bad music, and various things like that. She also used to play the piano; I don't remember anything she played, probably because it wasn't good at all (Nah, she played rather well for her age, playing at various concerts at these rather well ornamented concerts.) I remember having a fearful fascination of the piano. I didn't dare touch it at all, always avoiding it like it was cursed. I don't think I ever pressed one key on that thing in my childhood. I never understood why I acted that way towards it; the piano just gave me a bad aura, I guess. My mother, I'm not sure how to describe her. She meant a lot to me then, more than anyone else, but I hardly knew her – her personality almost indescribable. I remember her being melancholic and solemn a lot. I am aware however that she was very interested in music. It was because of her that I listened to my very first song, "In My Life" by The Beatles. But apart from these few facts, I barely knew her at all. My Dad was also the same, quiet, never really said anything to me, yet he also had this opposite side, this raging monster which erupted at any time, where he just lashed out against everything, me mostly. He, like my mother, was interested in music, but perhaps more deeply than she was. He wanted to be an opera singer when he was younger and once I saw a picture of him as a teenager playing guitar in the little farmhouse he lived in. That dream, of course, never came to fruition, but at night whenever there was a concert with a Asian performer, he would always sing along in this deep, strong, baritone voice, like Jim Morrison from the Doors.

We didn't have a lot of money and were in a lot of financial trouble. My Dad wanted to start his own business, contrary to my Mom who just wanted to start out slow and work in other people's businesses. But my Dad was a prideful man; he may have come from a farm, but he had forged a prosperous future for himself back in Asia. But now, he came to this country, for reasons my parents won't tell me, and he wanted to do things his own way. So, he then made the second biggest mistake of his life (the first I'll describe later): borrowing money. He borrowed money from the bank, from his friends, from his own family, and started his own business, which was a spa. However, business was small, and he didn't make a lot of money.

Pressure was starting to build up from everywhere, from the bank, from the people he borrowed money from, and he spent all his time and money trying to pay back the money he had borrowed. My Mom started growing resentful of him and kept arguing with him about the state of affairs he brought upon the family. They fought every night, screaming, yelling, throwing silverware and dishes at each other. The aftermath of their fights would be glass rubble littering the floor like the after effects of a battle, and my Dad would be off in the night in his car trying to cool off while my Mom would sit on the steps outside the house trying to find some solace in the silent moon above. Soon things got to be too much and she just left. There were no goodbyes or anything, she just left. Now you may be thinking that I grew resentful of my mother and doted on my father but that's only half true. I did grow angry at her leaving, but more than that I absolutely hated my father. He was like tyrant, a dictator, a person whom I couldn't escape from. His situation would stress the hell outta anybody's mind but the way people deal with that stress is different; most of the time he dealt with it by watching TV and, other times, on me or my mother in some cases. I don't really want to describe it but let's just say he would have made Jake LaMotta proud.

My mother, though she was always at work with my father and was never at home, I always viewed her as my protector. My parents slept in separate rooms, my Mom in the bedroom and my Dad in the living room. I slept in the living room as well but I was so scared by the thought of sleeping in the same room as my father that I would always slip into my Mom's room and sleep in her tired arms. Sometimes she would sing me a melody which I don't remember, but I remember the effect as being relaxing and sleep inducing. I loved my mother more than anything, but she just left. And that was that.

Life in the Bronx wasn't as bad as I make it seem. I was well connected with everyone living there. My sister and I knew everyone on our street, and we were close friends with these two kids, Violet and James. We played together a lot, doing a lot of crazy things. I remember one time James accidently ran over me with a bike, and I blacked out for a moment. I had a habit of losing consciousness as a child, didn't I? Well, anyway, I wasn't seriously injured so it was all good. My aunt owned this Italian market just a few blocks from where we lived, and my sister and I spent a lot of time there during the summer. Our cousins were almost there everyday, and we would do various things, like helping out at the market or doing something in my house. After helping out at the market, I always got free snacks, which were a delight. My aunt also used to hold these Italian-style banquets at her house during the summer, and she invited various members of our family and her friends there. The food was, of course, spectacular; probably the best Italian food I ever ate in my life, especially the meatballs.

My cousins, my aunt's children, had the typical sibling relationship: They absolutely detested each other. My cousin, Evelyn, had similar interests with my sister, but she was much spunkier and very weird. My other cousin, Patrick, was the typical male stereotype, infatuation with sports, tough, played a lot of video games, and was very rough. He used to push me around a lot but mostly acted like a big brother to me, I guess. My uncle though was something of a character, compared to the rest of my family. My Dad was a clean-shaven and well-dressed man, but my uncle was the polar opposite. He had a dirty unkempt appearance, a beard on his face, hobo style clothing, smelled of cheap beer and bad cigarettes, and loved golf and hunting, the two favorite past times of upper-class men, which was ironic considering how he dressed and acted. He was cool, though, having all the positive humorous aspects of a drunk and none of the negative alcoholic ones.

I still remember vividly the atmosphere of the Bronx during the summer. When it rained during the summer, the hot, soaking rain steamed streets, and sometimes a ghostly fog came up, blinding the vision. And at other times the rain would create this extremely hot and misty air that just soaked through your skin and made you feel like you were part of the Savanna. The ice cream truck would sometimes go through the neighborhood and kids would race out of their houses with pocket change in their hands and hungry eyes filled with murderous intent at the thought of ice cream melting in their sticky mouths. When my Mom was still around I would always go to the Bronx Zoo with her. My favorite exhibit was the lions. I was always fascinated with the king of the jungle for some reason, their majestic, regal appearance stimulating my untapped imagination.

I spent most of my time in the house though, never really going out. My best friend and only companion in my youth were probably the movies. My parents were almost never home, working from 7am to 9pm everyday, 7 days a week. And my sister was usually off at some friend's house, probably to escape the depressing situation at home. So I was stuck in the house all alone all the time. We had this huge cache of videos filled with all different kinds of movies from the contemporary, the weird, to the classics. My favorite film during my childhood was probably *Rumble in the Bronx* by Jackie Chan and the Disney movies *Cinderella* and *Snow White*.

Rumble in the Bronx was just plain ass-kicking awesome, especially the scene where Jackie Chan jumped from one building to another. Jackie Chan was probably the first person I regarded as a hero of some sorts, his action sequences just pure exhilaration. And regarding the Disney movies, well I came from a generation of kids that grew up on Disney and worshipped the movies as if they were the Bible, so it's understandable that some of the Disney films would be my favorites. I guess, I was a bit different from other kids, however, because I never watched the Disney movies that came out during the 90's like *Lion King* or *The Beauty and the Beast*. I watched the really, really old and classic Disney like *Snow White*, *Cinderella*, and *Alice in Wonderland*. I find it rather interesting that Cinderella had this rather provocative scene for a children's film, where Cinderella got undressed for a shower. Of course, we never saw the "details" but I think that was the only scene in Disney that hinted of nudity.

We also had the classic film, *Birds* by Alfred Hitchcock. I couldn't really describe the emotion I felt when I saw it. It was not the real, heart-thumping terror like that induced by the horror thrillers of the 90's, but rather this cold chill I just felt when the birds attacked the people.

As a child I was never really frightened by scary movies, but that film was the first time I actually felt fear. The ending where the people come out of the house and are just silently watched by the birds is particularly memorable for me. My heart was just in this suspended state waiting for something to happen, but it never did. The suspense and fear from that film was incredible though, and I avoided that film for a very long time. I think I had a few nightmares from it too. It was perhaps the first emotional experience I ever felt for a film. I mean, in the other movies, like *Rumble in the Bronx*, I was just in awe because of the action scenes, but that was just entertainment. This was something else, something deeper, and something much more intangible. There were also more emotional scenes from other movies. I remember in this one scene, I never figured out what movie it came from, but there was this man in this cave. And he was just lying there, downtrodden and beaten, and there was this blinding, ethereal, angel hanging over him and comforting him with some words from a gentle, sweet, and whispery voice. I was rather enamored of this image; there was just something mystical about it, I guess – something sacred like paintings of stories from the Bible. Sadly, to this day I never figured out what movie that scene came from.

Film obviously had a big effect on me as a child, but music, not so much. I remember watching the first rock concert I ever saw on TV, and I was frightened by it. Somehow, I got it into my head as a kid that rock music was the devil's music and watching that performance just scared the hell outta' me. Perhaps I got it from all the nuns at my school. It wasn't just rock music, I was frightened by anything musical, even the piano we had in my house. My sister played on it all the time but I was just afraid to touch it. I felt like only a few people were worthy of touching the piano, and I, of course, wasn't worthy of it. So, music never had a big effect on me, in contrast to my parents, who adored it, especially my father, the wannabe opera singer.

I went to the St. Francis of Assisi Catholic School for my education. Every morning, we would have to file into the gymnasium and have an assembly, where we said the pledge, led by the principal of the school, an old dying nun who looked like a walking corpse, rather than something that was really alive. Classes were rather typical of urban schools: unruly, troublesome kids, uncaring teachers, and just a chaotic environment in class. I was one of the nicer and quieter kids in my class. I never disrupted the teacher, said things out loud, or anything. But I never did any of the work either, and I failed all my quizzes and tests. School never interested me or held my attention as a child; my mind, more into the interesting world of the imagination. I never acted the same way to kids, always acting as a different person to different people for some reason. There was this girl, who absolutely hated my guts for some reason. To get her to like me I always used to act like a clown, performing absolutely terrible slapstick humor that would have made Charlie Chaplin ashamed, but she still always laughed. I kept tripping, falling, and hitting myself at random times just to make her laugh, and it worked. However, she still acted like she didn't like me, so all my work went to waste. I was really good friends with this kid, named Danny, a big kid for his age with cool spiky hair. He always made me touch and feel his hair for some reason, but it felt pretty cool so I never really minded. We played tag together a lot during recess and generally had a good time together. There was also this weird kid I was friends with, named Paul. He was a kid intensely interested in drawing and carried a drawing book with him wherever he went. I always requested various drawings from him, usually cartoon characters or such. He was damn good, and I was amazed at his work, which usually consisted of a Digimon or Pokemon character. At that age, stuff like that was our life, so what did I know about the aesthetics of art except what I considered was cool and hip?

Apart from school life, I also had a church life. When my grandma was living with us, I always used to go to the church with her on Sundays. It was an all Asian Catholic church, and it was where I was baptized as a baby. During the service everybody sang along with the priest but I never paid attention to that. There was this giant fresco that covered the entire ceiling, which captured my attention and mind. There were images of babies with wings, angels, holy figures, saints, all of the classic Christian imagery – all there in the ceiling, in all its glory and sacredness. It was the first painting I ever saw in my life, and because of the vastness of it, I was enveloped in its beauty. It wasn't like looking at a normal painting, which is always attached to the wall. This one covered the entire ceiling. It wasn't just a normal painting anymore, or just some other work of art, it was like a gateway to some holy image of the faraway past, imagination, or an unopened door in the soul. It was like there was a real heaven above us, hovering over us, a place untouchable by potentially sinful human hands. I was never really a religious person, and I always viewed that fresco as a testament to art, not religion, but regardless of my views on it, it always had this strange enrapturing power on me that never swayed even till today.

After my Mom left, things in the home went rather uneventfully until one day, when I was seven years old, we moved out of the Bronx and into Chappaqua. I was never aware of it; one day my aunt and uncle came, put me in their car, and, there, I was saying goodbye to the place I called my home until then. It was all so sudden; I don't think my mind has fully processed it, and only when high school started, I was beginning to feel the effects of abandoning my hometown, a feeling I don't feel comfortable in describing. My family didn't have any money and my Dad wanted to get the hell out of the Bronx, so my aunt agreed to let him move in with her in her house at Chappaqua. It was a big house, so it could accommodate all of us. My sister slept in my cousin, Evelyn's room, while my father and I got one room together. When we first moved there, we were like the immigrants of 19th century America. The room was extremely bare, tiny, and dirty with a small bed and blankets, the only furnishing in sight. My dad and I didn't bring any of the clothes up, yet, so we wore only what we carried on our backs. It was all very hobo-like.

After my move to Chappaqua nothing really eventful happened. I can compress all my feelings and reactions to Chappaqua in three words: lonely, alienated, and repressed. The kids and people here lacked the energy, life, and uniqueness that the people in the Bronx had. Sure people down there were a lot poorer, but they had a quality of life that could only be gained through the hardships of reality and experience. People down there were well connected, knew each other; I felt like everybody was a part of a family down there. And I was born there as well; it was my rightful home and heritage, the rich tradition of the city passing on its history and lessons unto an innocent kid, finding his raison d'être in the steel canyons of the Big Apple. But I was rudely torn away from that place, like a child separated from his mother's milk, and forced into a place where I felt I never really belonged, not because of my race or any aesthetic reasons like that, but just something deep in the core of me that kept telling me that I have real home somewhere else which isn't here and never will be. When I was a kid, I never really felt any repercussions from being forced to leave the Bronx, but ever since high school, there has been this unsettling feeling all the time, like an itch deep inside where your fingers will never reach and where only your mind can see but never affect.

But enough of my personal issues, there are some rather interesting stories that occurred during my time in Chappaqua.

My Mom and Dad got back together when I turned 10. Apparently they were planning it for a while but not until my Dad's financial situation got better and my Mom saved up enough money. Was I ecstatic about it? No, but I wasn't really angry or resentful towards my mother. I was rather unemotional about this event. Why? I couldn't really say; I guess, ever since my Mom left, there's been a multitude of women coming in and out of my life, playing the mother role for a few months and then quickly leaving, like they never happened or I never mattered. I guess, I got so used to this that my real mother became like these other women, and I just felt unemotional towards her. When I was just a child, she was my guardian angel against the terrible forces of my father. Now…I don't know what she is to me. I still don't know. It was after she came back that I learned of some traits of her that I never really saw as a child but I started to realized now, such as her unreliability. She wasn't like those strong independent women, who forged their own path in life regardless of men. She was rather helpless, unable to do anything, always making mistakes, and dropping things or breaking stuff. It kind of ruined my image of her as a child. I just grew disillusioned with it, and I sort of distanced myself from her. Well, I don't really want to discuss this anymore, on to another story.

This one story actually happened in Queens, not Chappaqua, but I guess it got started in Chappaqua. There was this worker in my Dad's spa, who went through a rather harsh experience. Her husband divorced her, took all her kids, and then kicked her out of her house. She was an immigrant so she was essentially homeless and had nowhere else to go or rely on. My Dad took pity on her and took her into our house when my Dad could actually afford a house and moved out of my aunt's place. She was like my mom in the sense she was rather melancholic and solemn, but perhaps more emotionally wrought. I remember hearing her crying every night and I guess I couldn't blame her after everything that happened to her. I believe that my Dad entered into a relationship with her, out of actual attraction or pity, but I suspect, the latter was the cause.

After a while my Dad got her an apartment in Queens, and she lived separately from us. My Dad went to visit her all the time to continue the relationship. But my Dad was a rather unfaithful man. He started visiting other women during this time, and he actually brought me along to one of his dates. She caught him in the act, catching him with another woman in this restaurant in Flushing, Queens. Let's just say she wasn't too happy at that. One day, when my Dad, my sister, and I came out of the supermarket in Flushing, Queens, we met her for the first time in awhile, and the first thing she did when she met us was punch my father. She started hitting him, slapping him, and cursing at him, screaming and acting like a banshee from hell. My sister and I quickly retreated to the car, while we watched my Dad deal with her. My Dad tried talking to her, but she wouldn't hear of it and kept on hitting him. Other people who were around just stared at them like it was some mad spectacle that was there for their sick, twisted entertainment. This went on for like half an hour until he finally just walked away from her and into our car. We drove away trying to forget everything that had just happened until a few minutes later, we felt something huge crash into our car. We turned around quickly, wondering what the hell was going on, and we saw through the back window the car that just hit us. Inside, we could make out that it was the same woman, but this time it was different; last time, she was just trying to hit my father. This time, she was trying to kill us. We quickly tried to get away from her, but she kept on chasing us and hitting us, from the back, from the side. I remember that when she hit us once on the side, sparks just shot out at the place of impact. It was like something from the movies, except it wasn't entertaining; this time, it was real and mind-numbingly scary. We finally lost her on highway, and when we returned home, we found out my Dad was bleeding in a few places. The car was damaged, but not too badly. Overall, we escaped that episode safely, but I was rather shaken by that event. I remember, after that happened, I started to become a lot more paranoid, developing several OCD tendencies and being extremely scared whenever I walked home from school, always looking back behind me, wondering if she would come back like a ghost from hell, haunting me for the rest of my life. I had a lot of nightmares of her, where she came and just killed everybody, too. By the time high school arrived, I grew out of it, thankfully.

The other traumatic event that occurred was the time when my cousin was raped. It wasn't my cousin, Evelyn; it was another cousin, Sara, who arrived in America a few years after I was born. She skipped out on college in Asia to experience the American dream. Too bad it didn't work out for her; she was rather poor and never had a lot of money. One day, however – my family isn't exactly aware of where or how – but, apparently, she was raped by someone. When my Mom and sister were in the city, together, they went looking for her to visit and found her at this church. Something was wrong, however. She kept staring at the wall and didn't respond to my Mom or my sister. She kept staring at blank space or talking to herself and she also grabbed onto this man and kept calling him her husband. It was rather obvious she suffered a mental collapse and, considering the way she hung on to the man and kept calling him her husband (she had been a virgin), we theorized that perhaps she was raped at some time. She also lived in a rough part of New Jersey, which added more probability to our theory. But anyways, my Mom quickly called my Dad who then chose to call me for some reason, screaming and yelling at me things that I couldn't really make sense of during that time. I didn't really understand what he was saying, but I knew something apparently had happened to my cousin. It was only after my Mom and sister brought her back to our house that I realized what had happened.

It was very strange, seeing her in that state. Before, she was energetic, funny, and, I guess, an outgoing girl. But now, her eyes were just completely vacant, and she was muttering some nonsense, which no one could understand, like a mentally ill patient, which she basically was at the time. And then, there was this man, whom I've never seen before, but she was clinging on to his arm and kept calling him her husband. Apparently he came all the way with my Mom and sister because she kept attaching herself to him. He left soon afterwards, and we were just sitting there wondering, what the hell had happened to her. The entire family from all over the state converged on that one night trying to take care of her. While my grandma was saying some prayers for her, my sister and I were talking about what could have happened to her. We knew she didn't have a lot of money, but we didn't think that was a probable cause. I never really knew the whole situation of what had happened down there in the city, when my sister found her – only little bits and pieces so my information was a bit complete, but it was my sister who said that she probably got raped by somebody. Because she knew about the situation much more than I did, I trusted her and still think now that that was the probably cause. We took care of her for a few days; her mind went down the hole and into Wonderland, but nothing really traumatic happened after that. We finally managed to get her into a mental hospital, and when her Mom came over from Asia, they went there together, and we never saw or heard from them again.

This wasn't the end of the crazy events, however. There was also the time, when my Dad almost died from appendicitis. For a long time, my Dad was feeling really uncomfortable and the area around his stomach started hurting a lot. He started going to the doctor a lot, but they could never diagnose his problem. I didn't notice this was happening though, because my parents kept it all a secret, and I was distanced from them a lot, never eating dinner with them or only seeing them 3 or 4 times a week. But one night, the situation turned serious. After a month of going to a doctor and never really curing his problem, his body couldn't handle it anymore and started going into shock. I remember slumbering peacefully when my Mom shook me out of my dreams and made me rush to Dad. I had no idea what was going on until I saw him.

His body was convulsing and shaking all over. He could barely speak, and his body just kept going out of control. I called the ambulance, and while my Mom was outside waiting for them, I sat there with my Dad. It was the first time I really spent time with him for a long time. It was a rather shaking moment. I felt kind of scared at what was happening, but I wasn't in total panic. I kept thinking that my Dad was actually dying and how should I feel about this. I never had a good relationship with him, never, but this event really put it to the test, and I had no idea how to react to it. Should I feel scared? Sure, I felt scared, but I didn't think I was scared enough. Should I start crying? Heh, my Dad beat the tears out of me a long time ago, and nothing could make me cry anymore, all thanks to him. I just sat there for what felt like an eternity, feeling lost, scared, confused, depressed, and everything evil rolled into one into this black miasma that threatened to ruin me completely that night. Thankfully, the ambulance came and we quickly rushed him to the hospital. Finally, the doctors thought to do something which they didn't think of for a month, which was to x-ray his stomach. He was complaining about stomach pains for a month, but they had never thought to x-ray it. Well, when they did it, they finally realized his problem was with his appendix, and they performed an emergency surgery. It all went well, and he recovered. A crisis was averted that day.

But, it brought forebodings about the future. Next time, something serious happens to my father, he's probably going to die; his body can't handle the exhaustion from work anymore. How would I feel about his actual death? I couldn't figure out my mess of emotions when he almost died. What would it be like when he actually died? I don't know. I really, really don't know. I doubt it's going to come so simply like the moment of clarity from the Death of Ivan Illyich. Perhaps, by then when I'm older, I'll have matured enough to handle it. Or perhaps his death will lead me down a more miserable path than when he was still alive. I'm not going to worry about it though. Why? Well, Dylan Thomas said it more eloquently than I ever will,

Korean Youth Transitions

Youth called to age over the tired years and asked,
"What have you found?
What have you sought?"
And Age answered through his tears,
"What you have found.
What you have sought."

"POOR, BUT HONEST"

Francis Won

My name is Francis Won (my Korean name is "Chung Bin Won" and this means "Poor, but honest") and I am very grateful for this chance to have my autobiography published in this book.

My father was born in the city of Donghae, which means "East Sea", located in the Gangwon province in the year 1961 on October 23rd (Gangwon province, otherwise known as Gangwon-do, is one of the nine provinces in South Korea; it has an area of 16,894 km²; it also has ten cities, thirteen counties, and a population of 1,592,000). My grandfather, Duk Gyu Won, was a police chief at the time, and he would always do his best to help out the townspeople whenever he could: he taught farmers who were illiterate to read as well as write, and he would also allow kids to play baseball on the field in front of the police station.

An historic event that happened during my grandfather's career was on October 1968, when 130 North Korean commandos unit crossed the border in an attempt to lead a resistance against the South Korean government. In order to protect the city, my grandfather was on constant patrol. The incident ended with 110 of the commandos killed, 7 captured and 13 escaping.

My grandfather's job forced him to move from town to town; because of this, my father does not remember too much about the city where he was born. His earliest childhood memory is from the time he spent at Taebaek Elementary School in the city of Taebaek, which is literally translated as "Great white", located in the Gangwon province.

Since my father's elementary school was a great distance away, my grandfather would take my father to his school on his motorcycle. For many years, this was a regular way of transportation. But this would soon come to an end on the year of 1972 when, after a serious accident with a car, my grandfather was hospitalized for several months, and my father was forced to take the bus to get to school. After the accident, my grandfather would suffer occasional pain even after the surgery he received on his leg, and my father would feel downtrodden because he felt that it was his fault. Starting from his middle school years at Taebaek Middle School and on, my father's method of transportation became a bicycle.

My father was very studious during his middle school years. He was top rank in his Honors class. His favorite subject was English, and he would spend his time memorizing English vocabulary. When my father wasn't studying, he was playing either soccer or table tennis. He also took Tae-Kwon-do classes, and reached the rank of black belt. During winter, he would skate on the frozen creek in front of his school. My father and his friends would also play with jaegi, which is a Korean traditional hacky sack, as well as sledding down hills. Hearing the accounts of my father's childhood made me realize that he too was once a kid looking to have fun, similar to how I was and still am.

Because Taebaek was a coal mining city, my father would always see miners hard at work. Taebaek would occasionally be referred to as "World's end" because of the hard living conditions the miners were under. Mines would frequently collapse, making the miners worry every single day about whether or not they would live to see the next day. This sort of melancholic life led many of these miners to become alcoholics, and they would frequently get into fights and in extreme cases, they would commit murders. Because he grew up watching the terrible way of life for these miners, as well as my grandfather's positive influence as a police chief, my father's childhood dream was to become a police officer or a soldier in the army, in order to protect his nation as well as to help the people who were suffering. My father had also felt that living a lawful life, helping others, would bring greater joy than a simple materialistic life.

But once my father had graduated from Taebaek High School, and was in the process of becoming a college student, his simple visit to Jesus Abbey, a small Christian community, changed his future goals.

Jesus Abbey, which was founded in the year 1965 by Father Archer Torrey, an Anglican Priest, with his wife Jane Torrey, was to be an experiment in Christian living, which Fr. Torrey had articulated into "the three labs" of the Christian life; the Christian's personal relationship with God, the Christian's relationship with other Christians, and the relationship of Christians (the church) with the world. My father went to Jesus Abbey for the first time at the age of 20, with Woo-jin Kim, his best friend, in the spring of 1980. The reason my father went to Jesus Abbey, was that he wanted to have a spiritual experience. It was there that my father became a born-again Christian. Since then, instead of pursuing a career as a police officer or a soldier, my father decided to live a Christian life of service in order to help people.

With this new goal, he decided to go to the Korean Anglican University of Seoul. The university, which was founded in 1914, was originally called St. Michael's Seminary with a purpose of training future Korean Anglican priests. It became the Korean Anglican University of Seoul (also known simply as Sung-kong hoe) in 1994. My father entered the university in 1982, but he was drafted into the army after the first three months, as it was the law and duty of every male Korean citizen to serve in the military for three years. During his military career, my father received a plaque for his exemplary service. After his military career was over, my father decided to return to his studies.

In the university, my father joined a band in which he played the bass in order to raise money to help the poor. The band, named Elpis (meaning hope in Greek), played gospel songs as well as Korean folk songs. As the General Secretary of the student council, my father helped promote student social well-being as well as organizing student conferences. When he graduated in 1989 and received his Bachelor's degree in Theology, he decided to return to Jesus Abbey to further his spiritual knowledge.

During his stay in Jesus Abbey, my father began to train for a monk-like lifestyle; he had been invited to a monastery in Australia. After his seven years of training, on January 1989 on New Year's Day, my father prayed to ask God if he should enter the monastery, or get married, or return to the theological seminary.

At this time, Hye Kyung Jang, my mother, had a dream during her stay at Jesus Abbey. In the dream my mother was throwing timber into the furnace to heat up a room, but the people inside still complained that it was cold. So, my mother closed the door on the furnace, then the people inside told her that it was very warm and started dancing. When my mother told Noah Jung, a youth teacher at Jesus Abbey, of her dream, he began to pray, and then told her to pray about a possible marriage.

A few months later, on February 14th 1989 my mother had just finished baking a cake for Mrs. Jane Torrey, the wife of Fr. Torrey (the founder of Jesus Abbey), and was carrying a bucket of hot water back to the lodging house so she could take a shower (there was no boiler to heat up the water). As my mother was walking down the stairs, she slipped and the water she was holding fell on her and she suffered second degree burns on her wrist. Because it was Lunar New Year, the hospitals were closed. Hearing of my mother's plight, my father went to Taebaek to purchase ointment; the reason for this is because my father lost his younger sister because she was scalded when she was at a very young age, and when a situation similar to my father's past happened to my mother, he was compelled to do whatever he could to help my mother. While he was nursing her back to health, my mother was very moved by his actions, and they fell in love and soon my father decided to give up on his plans to become a monk.

After a few years of consideration, my father worked up the courage to propose to my mother, and when she realized her prayer was answered, she agreed. Their marriage was on November 11th, 1989, at the St. Thomas Anglican Church in Seoul, and numerous people attended.

Both my mother's family and my father's family attended as well as people from Jesus Abbey. My father's colleagues and friends from his university also attended the wedding.

I was born a year later on September 4, 1990. I had the misfortune of being born feet first which would have led to my demise, had my mother refused the doctor's recommendation for a Caesarean section to get me out. For that I am eternally grateful to my parents, especially my mother for ruining her own body to save her son.

Two years after my birth, my family decided to move to the village of Bonghwang. Bonghwang is well known for being the location of the Samil Movement (pronounced "Sahm il" which is literally translated as "three-one", because of the date the movement, which took place on March 1st, 1919). This is the earliest displays of Korean independence movements during the Japanese rule of Korea (1910-1945). The core of the movement was gathered at Taehwagwan Restaurant in Seoul, and the movement began with the reading of the Korean Declaration of Independence, which was written by the historian Choe Nam-seon and the Buddhist monk Manhae. Soon the movement spread all across the nation, and people began to gather in large crowds, which led to the Japanese having to call in the army as well as the navy. The movement was brutally put down with 7,509 killed, 15,849 wounded, and 46,303 arrested, with many of the arrested people being taken to the infamous Seodaemun Prison in Seoul where they were imprisoned without trial and tortured.

The reason for our sudden departure to Bonghwang was that my father wanted to continue to pursue a career as a priest for the Anglican Church as he had decided when he was at Jesus Abbey.

In the years 1992 to 1994, my family lived at Bonghwang, located in South Chungcheong province, in poverty, with barely a morsel to eat. To support the family, my father worked in the fields with Gabriel Lee, one of the farmers, just so we could have a bite to eat. We couldn't afford coal to burn in the furnace to keep our house warm, and so we would spend parts of winter in the cold. If not for the generosity of Daniel Lee, one of the fellow villagers who owned a cucumber farm, we would have frozen to death in the extreme coldness of winter.

My father's life on campus at St. Michael's Seminary was very mechanical: he would wake up in the morning at 7 o'clock to attend the morning services; after breakfast he had studies until lunch. After lunch was more studies, then before dinner at 5 o'clock in the evening was an evening prayer, followed by dinner, then it was lights out. After two years of this lifestyle, my father graduated from Saint Michael's Seminary in Seoul. My father was then called by The Rt. Rev. Paul Yoon, the bishop of the Daejeon Diocese, to the city of Daejeon, which, literally translated, means "large fields"; then, he was summoned to the Daejeon cathedral. It was here that my father became a deacon for the cathedral.

Daejeon is the fifth largest city in South Korea, with a population of 1,442,856. It has an area of 539.84 km^2 and is located in the Chungcheong province. It is comprised of 5 districts and is home to the Daedeok Science Town, which is an area with more than 200 research institutions.

During our life in Daejeon in the year 1994, there was a time when I had gotten lost when I decided to go for a walk by myself. I had decided to go for a walk around the city without informing my parents, and needless to say, I got lost very quickly. I was in such a foreign surrounding with so many unfamiliar faces. Fear and despair overtook me and I broke down and began to cry.

Luckily for me, a stranger walked up to me and asked me what was wrong and I managed to get my message across through all my sobs and mumblings. When he asked me where I lived, I told him that I did not know my own address, and that all I could remember was the name of the church that my family was attending. Once the stranger heard the name of my church, he carried me on his back and began to head towards the church. After a few minutes of walking, I saw my parents standing outside a very familiar building; I soon realized that it was my house (I had completely forgotten that the church was just around the corner to the house). When my parents saw me, they rushed over and began to comfort me. Not fully realizing what was going on, I began to cry once more. The man explained to my parents what had happened, and my parents thanked him numerous times, and although I can't remember the man's name or face, I will never forget this act of kindness for as long as I live.

One year had passed when my father was finally called to become a priest, and my family was once again forced to move to the village of Dunpo, which is literally translated as "harbor barracks", in the year of 1995. During our stay at Dunpo, which is a farming city consisting of a population of roughly 12,000, my father would assist the farmers with their works by day, and at night would pray for them as well as having Bible studies at the church.

While we lived in Dunpo, a disaster stuck. The house owned by a widow that was just down the hill from our church caught on fire. When the fire was put out, there was nothing left of the house. She had lost everything she owned in the fire, and my father felt compelled to do something to help her. My father contacted the Korean Anglican Church and requested for their assistance. After praying day and night, his prayer was answered, and we received the aid of the KAC. The house of the widow was rebuilt, and because of my father's willingness to help, the widow was greatly moved and began to attend our church.

The History of the Korean Anglican Church begins on November 1st, 1889 when Charles John Corfe, who was summoned by the Archbishop of Canterbury, was consecrated to be the presiding bishop in Korea. Bishop Corfe gathered people who were willing to go serve in a foreign nation, and set sail for Korea. The bishop and his followers arrived on September 29th, 1890 at Incheon port. Bishop Corfe then opened a number of educational institutions, medical facilities and social work centers across the country, such as the Sinmyeong (Faith and Enlightenment) schools and the hospitals in the vicinities of Incheon, Yeoju and Jincheon as well as the orphanages in Suwon and Anjung. The missionaries also sought for ways for the church to be integrated into Korean culture. As a result of that effort, there are several Anglican Church buildings which were constructed in the traditional Korean architecture and which survive today, such as Seoul Cathedral, which was established in 1890.

In addition, the early missionaries made pioneering contributions to Korean studies. The first Korean bishop, The Rt. Rev. Paul Lee, was consecrated in 1965. Since the 1970s the Anglican Church has increasingly expanded through opening a number of new churches across country. The Church has been active in constructing new church buildings, along with its continued efforts in opening the new additional churches since the mid-1980s. The Provincial Constitution of the Anglican Church of Korea was declared on September 29, 1992, and the first Korean primate was inaugurated on April 16, 1993, and the Church finally became an independent national church with its commitment to sharing renewed life with the people.

After three years of service in the Dunpo Saint Thomas Anglican Church, our family moved to Canada in the year of 1999. The reason for this sudden move to a foreign nation was so that my father could earn his Doctor's degree in theology at the Wycliffe College in Toronto, Canada. But when my father found out that a Korean church in Toronto was struggling because they lacked a priest to guide them, my father put his studies aside and decided to work full-time for St. Timothy's Korean Anglican Church.

Because the church lacked funding, and could not fully support our family, my mother was forced to work part-time at a post office. Although my mother's body was weak from the numerous surgeries she had to undergo, she still worked hard to support our family as well as teach the Sunday school at the church. Our family lacked a method of transportation during the first year, and my father was forced to take public transportation to visit the members of the church.

During one of my father's many visits to a member, the bus driver suddenly told my father to get off the bus without any reason whatsoever. My father was forced to get off at a foreign location. Not being able to speak fluent English, my father was not able to object to this sudden incident that can only be described as a discriminatory act. My father wept tears of sorrow at such a hateful act, and began to feel the weight of being in a foreign nation fall upon his shoulders, but remembering that he must stay strong for the sake of our family's future, he shook off his despair and continued his works for the church without complaint.

Besides his church works, my father also worked with Canadian-Korean Children's Association which worked with kids that were adopted into Canada from

Korea, and taught them of their Korean backgrounds. My father taught the children Korean culture as well as help them to visit their original hometowns in Korea.

Looking back on my life, my fondest memories are of when I was still living in Canada. I remember having to live in the basement of my aunt's house for the first two months of my life in Canada, because we weren't able to find a house to live in right away. While we stayed in my aunt's house, I used to play around the fireplace a lot; throwing in newspaper and other useless scraps of paper to pass the time. It was also at this time that I started to teach myself English by reading books, such as Clifford the Big Red Dog, and by watching television shows, like the Magic School Bus.

Although I lacked comprehension, I began to understand what letters produced what sounds, and when I started to attend Hollywood Public School, the local elementary school, in 1999, as a third grader, I was able to further my understanding of the English language, thanks to the ESL program and the great teachers I had.

Elementary school was very eventful for me; it was where I learned to bake pies, where I made my first friends, and where I learned French. To my disappointment, the French language was harder to pick up than the English language, and the fact that I had joined the class half-way through the year's lessons did not help me in any way. Nonetheless, I did not give up and tried my best to learn French on the side while learning English as well.

When I joined the cooking class to learn to bake pies, I was surprised to find out that I was the only guy in the class. At first it was awkward, but once we started baking things, it quickly became fun. Thanks to that class, I later on gained an interest in cooking, and I decided to teach myself how to cook simple dishes like spaghetti, omelets, as well as numerous other foods.

Since my family lacked an automobile, as well as my parents refusing to let me walk to school at such a young age, my father would give me a ride on a bicycle to my school. This continued until I was in the fifth grade. I was embarrassed at the fact that I had to ride a bike to school, let alone the fact that my father was the one who was giving me a ride. I was always envious of the kids that would come to school by car, but not wanting to disappoint my father who went through such trouble, whether it was raining or snowing, I kept my feelings of embarrassment to myself. Reflecting back on this however, makes me realize that I should be very thankful for what my father did, as he decided it necessary for him to take the time out of his day to take me to school on a bicycle as well as taking me back home. I realize how hard it must've been for him to do that day after day, year after year, and I wonder if I would have enough commitment for me to do that for my kids.

After graduating from Hollywood Public School in 2001, I moved up to Steelesview Public School located in the northern part of Toronto. Although I was happy that I was finally in sixth grade, I was disappointed that my address forced me to go to a school away from my previous friends.

I had missed my friends since I had spent years with them in elementary school playing games and having fun. It was especially harder for me since they were the first friends I've gained in Canada. They were the ones who had shown me around the school, and they were the ones who began to talk to me although there was a language barrier. I began to miss my friends that I had gained, and began to feel alone, despite the fact that I began to make friends at my new school.

When I told my parents of my woes, my parents tried their best to find a place we could move to so that I could change schools. It took a couple of months, but I was finally able to go to Bayview Middle School which was located in North York, Ontario.

It was at Bayview Middle School that I was first exposed to an instrument other than a recorder. The school was offering instruction in a variety of woodwind as well as brass instruments. Although I had originally wanted to play the alto saxophone, I eventually settled with the tenor saxophone. Although I had thought that I would stick to just the tenor sax, my indecisive personality caused me to switch between multiple instruments. This led to me not being able to join the school band which I greatly regret now.

Through the curriculum offered at the school, I also learned to make things during shop class, and I learned to type properly for the first time during computer class. Looking back, middle school is full of memories that I still cherish and I miss the friends that I had made during my middle school years.

But middle school is only full of good memories; it was also during middle school when I started to become obese. My lack of exercise as well as my growing disinterest in sports began to cause fat to build up in my body, and soon I became overweight. Initially I had no idea that I was slowly becoming fat, but once my classmates began to ridicule me, I finally realized that I had become fat. Despite all the insults I received, I remained passive on the matter and decided not to take action. By the time I was in seventh grade, I was 182 pounds with the height of 5'6 ft. Although my parents continuously warned me of the consequences of being overweight, I paid no heed until the end of my seventh grade year.

When I was fourteen years of age during the year of 2004, I felt frustrated by the fact that I couldn't speak Korean, as well as feeling bad about myself because I was constantly ridiculed for my obesity. And feeling the need for a fresh start before the next school year, I talked to my parents and decided to spend an entire summer vacation in Korea visiting relatives and friends with my mother as well as staying at my childhood home, Jesus Abbey. My mother decided that we should visit the Diocese of Daejeon, to meet my father's peers such as Kim Ho-wook, whom I had always called "uncle" as I was growing up. When we arrived at the diocese, we were greeted by many familiar faces. My father's peers commented on how much I had grown as well as how obese I had become. After talking for a short while, my mother and I were invited to join the celebration of the 40th anniversary of the Daejeon diocese; they also requested that I say some congratulatory words in English for a video that they planned to play while we ate. The celebration began with a service that was led by The Rt. Rev. Andrew Shin, the bishop of Daejeon; then, we moved to the lower floors of the cathedral and began to eat lunch. I went outside for a breath of fresh air, so I missed most of the events that took place. After the lengthy farewells I headed for Jesus Abbey.

During my stay at Jesus Abbey, I was not only able to grow spiritually, but also to grow physically fit. The motto at Jesus Abbey was, "Work is prayer; prayer is work". This motto is derived from the Benedictine tradition of work and prayer. Following this motto, I was to participate in a range of labors, from working in the fields to completely demolishing and renovating a bathroom. Though I did these labors while having an endless list of complaints, I always had a sense of fulfillment when the project was done. The biggest sense of accomplishment I had was when I helped sanding an entire playground so that the younger kids may play on it without the worry of getting splinters. The process was difficult because I had to use a small sander to do the job, and it took around 2 or 3 days to complete the job, but once it was finished I felt a feeling of accomplishment in my heart. Although the labors were difficult for a person of my age, I was happy to take part in something that my parents had to do during their stay at Jesus Abbey.

After a couple of weeks, my mother headed back to Canada to assist my father at church, and I agreed to stay behind alone.

While I stayed in Jesus Abbey, I experienced numerous things that I wouldn't have had, had I decided to stay in Canada. I was able to take part in the conference for North Korean missions, during which I was able to see the hardships that North Koreans had to suffer, as well to have the privilege of watching a North Korean movie. The documentary movie was only a couple of hours long, but it was enough to see the North Korean way of life as well as their way of thinking. The movie was about a North Korean man trying to pass a test in order to become a worker. The test consisted of picking up dirt using a shovel and then tossing the dirt accurately through a hoop. The first time he tried the test, he failed miserably. It was also at this scene that I was allowed to see a North Korean way of portraying humor. The dirt he tossed hit the judge in a manner that could be described as slapstick comedy. Although there were various things I disagreed with – such as the portrayal of communism as being the best form of government, as well as endless praises of their "Dear Leader" Kim Jong il – the film itself was, to my surprise, fairly enjoyable. The conference, which took place in Jesus Abbey, went on for a few more days with speakers (I can't recall their names), coming in to tell us, how difficult it is for a missions program to succeed in a communist country.

After three months of stay at Jesus Abbey, it was time for farewells. Although on the surface I put on an act to make it seem as though I was glad to leave, I felt a small tug at my heart for having to leave my peaceful childhood home.

Once I left Jesus Abbey, I stayed with relatives until it was time for my flight back to Canada. During the flight I was able to reflect on the things that had happened during my stay in Korea and how it had made me a more mature person. Despite my complaints, I had learned a lot from my short stay in Korea, and I gained a better grasp of the Korean language, and I felt that my trip was well worth the three months of labor I went through.

When I arrived at Pearson Airport in Toronto, I rushed off the plane and claimed my bags. I hadn't seen my parents in three months, so I was eager to see them. After going through customs I went through the arrival gate and immediately spotted my father and began to run towards him. To my disappointment, my father did not recognize me. During my stay in Korea, I had dropped 24 lbs of weight, and my hair had grown down to my shoulders. As my father began to walk away, I felt a sudden sense of panic, until my mother greeted me. Despite my changed appearance, my mother had instantly recognized me and ran over to hug me. I was finally reunited with my family, and I had never felt happier. Ignoring my feelings of disappointment, I greeted my father and we got into our car and headed home. Although I initially had complained to my father about him not recognizing me, I soon let it go and only mentioned it when I got into trouble or during conversations that put me at a disadvantage.

My stay in Canada was coming to an end, as my father was being transferred to a church in New Jersey in the spring of 2006, which meant that we had to leave the church in Toronto and its members. After seven years of hardships, hard work and many days of prayer as well as my service of seven years as an acolyte assisting my father during mass, the church that originally had twelve members in the beginning was revitalized and the attendance had steadily grown to the size of 70 members. My family had grown attached to the church in the seven years that we had attended as well as its members, and needless to say, our farewells were full of tears. We were saddened that we had to leave the people who had become like family to us behind, but I began to look forward to living in America. I had only been to America on visits, and was always interested in living in America had I been given the chance, and for my wish to come true left me dumbstruck. We soon boarded the plane headed for the place that I would soon call home.

We arrived in New Jersey in the month of April 2006, and my father was put in charge of a Korean Episcopal church in North Bergen, NJ. I felt out of place when I first arrived, and although the place felt similar to Canada, the little differences made it hard to adjust at first. One of the main things that became an annoyance for me was that I had grown used to calling the restrooms "washrooms" in Canada instead of "bathrooms" as is the convention in the USA. I was ridiculed by my friends for being from Canada ("do they really say 'eh?' at the end of all their sentences?") but was able to blend with the crowd after the first few months. Although my new friends at church teased me for being from Canada, they helped me fit in, and thanks to their warm welcomes, I soon felt right at home. I finally adjusted to my new home, and I had time to gain a few hobbies as I had arrived near the end of the school year.

One of the hobbies I picked up was art, and it was also around this time that I gained an interest in music and guitars. I developed a strong interest for playing guitar after watching a video of a guitarist who called himself Kurikinton Fox, performing a song on Youtube around 4 years ago. Before then I never saw the appeal of playing the guitar; I had tried taking acoustic guitar lessons from my father, but never really got into it as I felt that I could use that time playing video games. But the video had made me realize how foolish my way of thinking was, and I became determined to learn to play the guitar. After much convincing, my parents finally agreed to buy me a guitar.

When I walked into the Guitar Center to pick out my guitar, the first one to catch my eye was the Gibson Les Paul. After trying out the guitar, the rich sounds it produced along with the appeal that the shape of the guitar produced immediately gave me the urge to purchase it. Then, my eyes saw the price tag of $2,500. I immediately set down the guitar, not wanting to get attached to it, and trying my best not to feel discouraged, began to look for a cheaper guitar. When I asked one of the employees, he recommended me the Yamaha Pacifica, which cost $200, along with a Fender amplifier. Although it was hardly the guitar of my dreams, I was satisfied to be holding an axe to call my own. After the purchase, I went home and decided to try out the guitar, and I was pleased with the sounds it produced. When one of my friends told me to play a song, however, the fact that I had yet to learn to play struck down my moment of joy.

Desperately wanting to play like the professionals did, I went to the nearest Barnes and Nobles to pick up a chord book as well as a practice book for beginners. After hours of practice, I had mastered the basic chords and knew them by heart. Feeling confident about the seven chords that I had mastered, I decided to try and play a song. To my surprise, I was horrible. I also did not know how to read music, which only made things more difficult. All the notes looked like a foreign language to me, and I was too prideful to ask my father to teach me something that I had once felt would be easy to learn. I had hit a wall and feeling lousy about myself, I put my guitar on its stand and soon forgot about it.

A whole year had passed when I felt the urge to play guitar again. I picked up my Pacifica, which had become rusty and dusty due to my negligence, and decided to play a song. I was amazed to learn that the basic skills that I had learned and trained were still somehow fresh in my mind, and that the songs that I had felt were difficult became easier the more I practiced them. With renewed confidence I began playing guitar again, and soon my repertoire of songs began to grow; I began by covering songs from bands such as AC/DC, Blink 182, and Foo Fighters. I was no longer barred by my lack of confidence for I had learned the valuable lesson that I could achieve anything through practice. I now play the guitar for my church once a month during a special song service, as well as play for special events, such as the Christmas "concerts" at church. I also take part in the church choir every Sunday as a bass singer. Although many people have discouraged me about dedicating my life to music, I still hold on to that flame of passion in my heart. I hope to one day join a band that I can dedicate myself to full-time.

To this day, my parents continue to work day and night fulfilling church duties; they visit the church members' homes to pray for them when they are sick, or when they are feeling melancholic about their life. They also helped a couple that had grown apart to find renewed love. I am proud to have parents who do their best to serve and help others, and I hope that I may be able to live my life as they do. I currently attend Hackensack Christian School, and am getting ready to go to college, and I hope I will be given the chance to follow through on the things that I had always wanted to accomplish, such as joining a band.

The school I currently attend, Hackensack Christian School, is located in Hackensack, New Jersey. The school is funded by the Baptist church that works along with the school administration. They offer courses such as Bible, as well as Drama. When I first began to attend the school, I was completely taken by surprise at the size of the school. The school that I had attended previously had 30 students in a single class. In HCS I was in a class of 13 students. At first I was unhappy with my being in the school. I began to question why I hadn't gone to a public school instead. My parents informed me that they thought it would be better for my spiritual growth to go to a Christian private school. I had many complaints while I was in school, ranging from the dress code, as well as the uniform, and occasionally about the members of the faculty. As time passed, however, I began to like the school more and more. I made plenty of friends during my high school career at HCS, and the teachers I've met are very nice. I am thankful to my parents for paying the tuition to allow me to continue going to the school. I hope to end my senior year with a bang.

Writing this autobiography has allowed me to reflect on my life and see the errors I've made, as well as my triumphs. It has given me a fresh outlook on life; as opposed to the negative attitude I had just a few months ago. I was able to change myself from one who was bored and tired of life to one who is looking forward to the future as well as to what it may bring. I am glad to have this opportunity to write an autobiography, as it will impact me for the rest of my life.

A TWIN

Dain Lee

Getting up early comes naturally to me because I was born at 7:00 a.m., and I've been getting up early for a long time. On October 28, 1991, I and my twin sister, Haein Lee, were born on a cool day in Seoul, Korea. When I was born, many interesting turns occurred, but the most significant event in my early childhood at the point I was born can be expressed as "stubbornness." Commonly, newly born babies immediately cry after birth, but I didn't cry. Furthermore, I had cut a tooth. It is abnormal to have a tooth for baby. While a dentist pulled out my tooth, I didn't cry as well.

Of course, I can't consciously remember anything from the first two or three years of my life after birth. Incidentally, I may say that I didn't have my own name for a month. My twin sister got a name because she was born right before me. It means that she's my elder sister so she could get a name earlier than me. At first, my parents were planning to give me the name of Sue-in, but Sue-in and prisoner are homophones in Korean. So my parents decided to use name that my mom's friend recommended, which is Dain and it means, "kind-hearted."

Before I and my twin sister were born, several unpleasant events have occurred because all my siblings are girls. At the time, there was a boy-preferring culture in Korea. Most families wanted sons, rather than daughters. Still, after we were born, we grew up with plenty of love. Especially, I was loved by my grandparents. I spent so much time with my grandparents – nearly 3 months of each year. My mother told me that she felt mistreated by me because I was so very attached to grandparents – more than to mother.

My twin sister and I were a little different. My sister was jazzy but I was a bashful child. Contrary to my visible characteristic, I was actually a naughty girl. One winter day of 1993 before my family moved to Hong Kong, I and my twin sister broke all eggs which were in the refrigerator and scrubbed all the eggs on the wall, clothes, and photos while my mother took a nap. When she woke up, she was shocked and cleaned up all alone the mess we had made. After my family moved to Hong Kong, I got into mischief as usual. My family dwelled in a high-rise apartment building. I don't know why I flung toys out windows. I think I felt choky because I had stayed at home all day. My mother picked up all the toys which were put in a bush with creepy bugs.

I was so young that I don't remember the days in Hong Kong very well. As my memory runs, life in Hong Kong was enjoyable. I encountered many cultures; it was a great experience that I had, and I remember dimly that I spoke in English for a short time. However, like most living in Hong Kong at a young age, I was almost always at home and in neighborhood playgrounds or swimming pools, etc. with my twin sister.

3 years elapsed and my family moved back to Korea and settled in Gooro, Seoul. I attended kindergarten and was stressed out by the hectic urban environment. I didn't know how to speak Korean and had clumsy expressions; I couldn't read or write Korean. I remember

that I went to a field trip which is going to teach students to learn traditional Korean decorum. One of the activities was to write a letter for parents. But I couldn't write any words while other kids were writing. It gave me great stress, and I made a gradual retreat.

Although I was a blunt but taciturn person, I had much self-respect and propelled myself to do something that I really wanted. It was violin. I teased my father to buy me a violin, since I saw my cousins playing violin and I was jealous of her. After that, I started to learn violin. I thought there was something attractive about violin. I fell in love with the glamour and soft sound of violin. I'm was not taught violin since I came to the U.S., but I play often whenever I want to play, using my skills acquired in the past. I participated in a string orchestra in school and played violin until last year, but I am playing viola this year. I haven't learned it from a viola teacher (I taught it to myself), but I'm doing my best. I am surprised that I try to learn something new because I wasn't a person challenged to do so by anyone. I feel pride about myself, however, because I perceived a little change in me.

After 2 years of living in Gooro, our family moved to Jamsil, Seoul, again and lived there until I was a 4th grader. At the age of eight years old, I met my best friend, Hyerim. I met my best friend in my life. We have been friends for quite a while now. We hang out together every time we can, and we share each other's sorrows or joys. End of 4th grade, my family moved to Gwangjoo, Kyungkido. At that time, I was so depressed because we had to be separated. But we met each other at least once a month and our friendship continued more amicably.

After I graduated from elementary school, I entered into Jang-ahn Middle School. I had hard time with studying. I was shocked about my mid-term grade in my first semester. My mother noticed that I was depressed about it and gave me an advice to take it easy. She always emphasized that relationship is more important than school work.

On June, 2006, my father announced that we were going to America, when I was studying for final exams. I was very excited at first, but I started to worry about how I could learn English which was my least favorite subject in Korea. My family arrived in America on August 26, 2006, with hopes.

My first school in America was McLean High School in Virginia. I faced a lot of problems. On the first day of the school, I and my twin sister couldn't understand any of words, so we even missed our first class. Every class, I was dependent on my dictionary. I always carried my dictionary and used it when I didn't understand what teachers said. Since I was in Korea, I have been a taciturn person. However, I realized that I had to stop being like a deaf-mute. My moody expression caused misunderstanding between me and my teachers. Teachers thought that I was worse than my twin sister because I didn't talk and express my opinion at all. So, I was put in a lower ESL class than Haein. Furthermore, the ESL teacher even told my mom to make an appointment with a doctor because she thought that I had a mental problem. My mom and I suffered a lot and cried almost every night.

After I finished the difficult freshmen year, I reluctantly changed schools to Langley High School because of the family move. Ironically, I made more friends at Langley High School than at McLean High School. However, I was still having hard time to catch up on the class work, especially in science. Every night before the tests or quizzes, I stayed up all night to study for the exams. Now, I can laugh about this, but I was very serious about this at the time.

While we had hard time in Virginia, my father relocated so our family came to New Jersey. Life in New Jersey was much easier for me to adapt to, and I realized that my English was improved. Also, I recognized that my own character turned more positive. I was hostile to unfamiliar things; however, I felt that I became an outgoing person, step by step.

I have to say that I was able to change to a very positive person with support and encouragement from my family and friends. I would like to be a medical doctor and volunteer in the 3rd world in return for their support and love.

For a difficult while, I couldn't speak proper English due to lack of confidence, I was regarded as a. mentally handicapped person, I was frustrated by something easily, and I was making somebody to feel shame because of my cold look. But now, I am changed. I had undergone some major changes during the past several years. And I'm also curious about my future.

My mom always told me that there's nothing impossible with God and that God did not send me to America to let me down. Even though these words don't affect me that much, I believe it, and I think that God will lead me.

나의 자서전

이다인

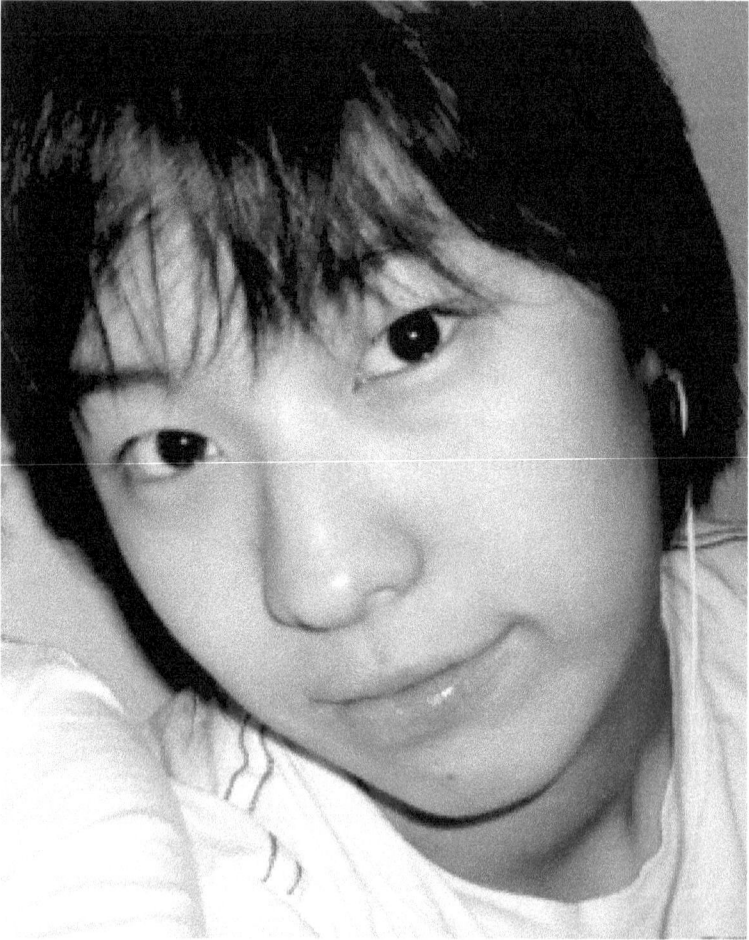

1991년 10월 28일 선선한 가을 날, 서울 잠실 중 앙병원에서 3자매의 막내이자 쌍둥이 중 동생으로 태어 났다. 뒤에 들은 이야기지만 난 태어나자 마자 참 이상

한 방법으로 나의 고집 센 면모를 드러냈다고 한다. 보통 아기들 같으면 뱃속에서 나오고 탯줄을 자르자 마자 울어야 하는게 정상인데, 난 전혀 울지 않았다. 내가 비정상적으로 이가 나서 뽑아야 했을때도 울음을 참느라 얼굴이 빨개졌던것을 의사선생님이 보시고 기가막혀 하셨다는 이야기를 훗날 엄마가 말씀 해 주셨다.

여담이지만, 나는 생후 한 달까지 이름이 없었다. 나보다 먼저 태어난 특권(!)을 누렸던 내 쌍둥이는 태어나자마자 '해인'이라는 이름을 가지게 되었지만, 미리 이름을 정해두지 않았던 부모님은 내 이름을 짓느라 한동안 고심하셨다고 한다. 가장 강력한 후보였던 '수인' 이라는 이름은 한국어 뜻으로 감옥에 갇힌 수감자를 연상시키는 이름이라 끝내 제외됐다. 내 이름은 어느 날 엄마의 친구가 추천해 준 '다인'이라는 이름으로 결정되었다.

딸이 셋이라 그런지 태어나기 전엔 여러가지 말 못할 사연이 있었으나, 태어난 후에는 많은 사람들의 사랑을 듬뿍 받으면서 자랐다. 친가 쪽의 사촌오빠들도 쌍둥이 형제였는데, 한 가족에 쌍둥이가 두 쌍이라는 사실이 참 신기했던 모양이다. 특히 나와 내 쌍둥이는 외할머니, 할아버지의 사랑을 듬뿍 받으면서 자랐다. 1년 중 거의 3개월 정도는 할머니 할아버지 집에서 살다시피 하고 또 홍콩에 가서도 여러번 한국에 들러 할머니 할아버지와 지냈던 것으로 기억한다. 엄마가 말씀해 주시길 할머니 할아버지의 사랑을 듬뿍 받고, 또 오랫동안 같이 지내서 그랬는지는 몰라도 어렸을 때는 외조부모님만 너무 따라서 서운해 하신 적이 있다고 하셨었다.

조금은 활발했던 내 쌍둥이와는 달리, 난 어릴 때

부터 고집은 조금 셌으나, 얌전하고 조용한 아이었다. 하지만 장난을 칠 때면 상상도 못 할 정도로 도가 넘는 장난을 쳤다. 1993년 겨울, 홍콩으로 발령나기 3달 전 즈음에 엄마가 우릴 돌보시다가 잠시 낮잠을 주무실 때에 나와 내 쌍둥이는 냉장고에 있던 계란들을 다 꺼내 온 집안을 계란범벅으로 만들고 다녔다고 한다. 그 뒷처리를 혼자 하셔야만 했던 엄마는 아직도 그 얘기가 나올 때 마다 고개를 젓곤 하신다. 나의 장난은 홍콩에 가서도 끊이지가 않았다. 높은 고층 아파트에서 살았던 나와 내 쌍둥이는 밖에 나갈 기회가 별로 없어서 답답했던지 베란다로 인형, 장난감 등등을 던져서 경찰이 와서 주의를 줬던 때도 있었고 또 나의 엄마는 징그러운 벌레들 사이에서 우리가 던졌던 인형을 울면서 찾아내셔야만 하셨단다.

홍콩에서의 기억은 너무 어렸을 때라 잘 기억은

나지 않지만 아주 즐거웠던 기억이 떠오르는 것 같다. 여러 문화를 접할 수 있었던 기회기도 하고, 아주 잠깐 이었지만 영어로 대화를 했었다는게 어렴풋이 기억이 난다. 하지만 대부분 홍콩에서의 생활에서의 나는 나이가 어려서 거의 집이나 놀이터 또는 수영장 등 동네에 안에서만 지냈던 기억이 난다. 그리고 유치원을 다니지 않아서 하루종일 내 쌍둥이와 시간을 보내야만 했다.

한국에 돌아와서는 바로 서울 구로동이란 곳으로 이사를 해서 유치원을 다녔다. 유치원을 다닐 때 한국어가 서툴고 한글을 몰라서 몹시 답답했던 적이 많다. 처음 유치원에서 간 수련회에서 부모님께 편지를 쓰는 시간이 있었는데. 한글을 몰라 한 글자로 쓰지 못했던 것이 기억난다. 그렇다고 영어를 잘 하는 편도 아니었기에, 내가 홍콩에서 왔다는 사실 하나로 아이들이 계속 나에게 영어로 말하는 걸 시켰을 때는 정말 어쩔 줄을 몰라했었던 기억이 난다. 나는 초등학교에 들어가기 바로 직전에 한글을 깨우쳤다. 보통 한국 애들보다 훨씬 느린 편인 셈이었다. 초등학교에 올라간 이후로 받아쓰기 시험을 볼 때마다 좋은 점수를 받을수 없었고, 안그래도 자신감이 없던 나는 점점 더 말을 아끼게 되었고 그에 따라 성격도 점점 무뚝뚝해져갔다.

내가 이렇게 말이 없고 무뚝뚝했었어도 자존심이 강했고 하고 싶은 일은 끝까지 몰아붙이는 경향이 있었다. 나와 약간의 라이벌 의식이 있었던 동갑내기 사촌이 바이올린을 켜는 걸 본 순간부터 아빠한테 바이올린을 배우게 해 달라고 끈질기게 졸랐고, 그렇게 해서 바이올린을 배우기 시작했다. 바이올린은 하면 할수록 즐겁고 한편으로는 연습하면 할수록 나날이 실력이 늘어가는 것이 신기했다. 지금은 바이올린을 배우고 있지는 않지만나 혼자 바이올린을 켜 볼 때마다 항상 색다름을 느낀다. 작년까지 나는 학교 스트링 오케스트라에서 바이올린을 켰었다. 하지만 이번 년도 부터는 바이올린과 비슷한 악기인 비올라를 연주하고 있다. 단 한 번도 배운적 없고 켜 본적 없는 내가 비올라를 켜고있다는 것 자체가 신기할 따름이다. 예전 같았으면 전혀 새로운 것을 시도해 보지도 않았을 내가 새로운 것을 찾아서 하는 나의 작은 변화를 보니 기분이 좋아짐을 느낀다.

　　　　서울 구로동에서 2년간, 유치원 시절과 초등학교 1학년 시절을 살다가 서울 잠실동으로 이사를 하고 초등학교 4학년 때까지 살았다. 초등학교 3학년 때는지금도 나의 베스트 프렌드인 혜림이를 만나게 되었다. 서로 한 동네 살면서 웃고 울며 많은 얘기를 나누었던 친구였다. 가정환경이 좋지못해 나에게 많은 고민도 털어놓던 친구였다. 초등학교 4학년이 끝나고 5학년이 되던 2001

년 겨울, 나의 가족은 또 한 번의 이사를 했다. 그 당시에 헤림이와 헤어지고 서로 다른 학교를 다닌다는 것은 정말 나에겐 슬픔이었다. 그렇게 아쉬움을 뒤로하고 떠나고 나서도 나와 내 쌍둥이는 거의 한 달에 한 번씩은 헤림이를 만나러 다녔었다. 서로 떨어져 지낸 기간동안 서로를 더 아껴주고, 더 보고싶어 한 덕분에 더욱 더 친해짐을 느낄 수 있었다.

초등학교 6학년 때, 나에게 아주 충격적인 깨닳음과 동시에 일이 하나 터졌었다. 너무나도 사랑하는 외할머니가 허리디스크와 함께 장기에 작은 혹이 생겨 큰 수술을 하셨기 때문이다. 할머니가 이미 꽤 많은 수술을 견디셨고 또 영원히 건강할 거라고 믿었던 나의 생각과는 달리 할머니는 많이 힘들어 하시고 거의 돌아가실 위기에 처할 뻔하였다. 할머니가 아프시기 전 까지는 나는 말로만 모태신앙인 내가, 할머니가 아프시고 나서야 눈물로 기도를 했던것 같다. 내 기도가 응답되었는지 할머니는 씻은듯이 나으셨다.

초등학교 때까지 평탄하고 즐거운 삶을 보내고 난 후 중학교에 입학했을 때 공부가 너무 어려워서 힘들어 했던 적이 많다. 중학교 입학 후 처음으로 봤었던 중간고사 점수를 받아보고 나서 너무나 충격을 받아서 마음고생을 많이 했었다. 하지만 엄마나 아빠는 늘 우리에게 많이 놀으라고 말씀하셨다. 그리고 지금 네가 노는 것이 나중에 후회없이 공부할수 있는 힘이 된다고 늘 말씀하셨다. 하지만 나는 학원도 잘 보내주지 않고 친구들과 사이좋게 잘 놀으라고만 하시는 엄마를 이해할 수가 없었다. 엄마아빠는 늘 공부보다 사람과의 관계가 우선이라고 말씀해 주셨다. 그 때 그 말씀이 이해되지는 않았지만 지금은 어느정도 이해가 간다. 나는 특히 과학과 사회공부를 하는 것을 좋아하게 되었다. 성적이 조금씩 오르고 친구들과도 좋은 친분을 유지할 수 있었다. 중학교 2학년이 내가 학교다녔던 생활 중에서 가장 행복했었던 시기인것 같다. 거의 모든 반 친구들과 어울려 친하게 지냈었고 또 담임선생님도 너무 좋았기 때문이다. 담임 선생님은 작은 일에도 늘 내게 칭찬해 주셨고 내가 멋있다고 격려해 주셨다. 마음에 우쭐하는 생각도 있었고 선생님 칭찬 때문이라도 더 열심히 공부하려고 했다.

2006년도 중학교 3학년 1학기가 끝나고 나서 아빠가 주재원으로 발령이 나서 우리 가족은 미국에 오게 됐다. 기말고사를 앞둔 6월의 어떤 날, 아빠가 퇴근하셔서 갑자기 우리가 미국으로 떠나게 되었다고 말씀하신 순간, 내가 알지 못하는 미국이라는 새로운 세계에 내가 살게 되었다는 사실에 날아갈 듯이 기뻤지만 한 편으로는 걱정이 밀려왔다. 영어를 잘 못하는 내가, 아니 배우는 과목 중에서 영어를 제일 못했던 내가 어떻게 미국에 가서 생활을 할 수 있을지 정말 막막했다. 그렇게 한국에서의 모든 것을 뒤로하고 2006년 8월 26일 오전, 나의 가족은 버지니아에 도착했다.

미국에 오고나서 거의 일주일 동안은 시차적응 때문에 아무데나 쓰러져서 잤었다. 그리고 할머니 할아버지와 헤어지고 와서 그런지 나와 엄마는 4일 동안 외조부모님 생각에 눈물을 쏟았다. 9월 4일 개학을 앞두고 나의 걱정은 미국에 오자마자 바로 닥쳐왔다. 아빠가 다니시는 은행 직원의 도움으로 학교에 갈 준비를 위해서 스테이플즈에 가서 각종 필기도구를 사려했었다. 새학기 전이라 그런지 인파가 많이 있었는데, 어떤 꼬마가

나에게 영어로 뭔가를 물어봤었던 기억이 난다. 아무것
도 알아듣지 못한 나는 그저 우물쭈물 거리다가 그 자리
를 떠났던 기억이 난다. 얼마나 부끄러웠는지.

미국에 와서 맨 처음으로 McLean High School이
라는 학교를 다니기로 시작했었다. 새학기가 시작되고
나서 정말 많은 어려움을 겪었었다. 첫 날 영어를 알아
듣지 못해서 나와 내 쌍둥이는 어디로 가야할 지 몰라
수업에 못들어갔던 기억이 있다. ESL에서는 선생님이
도대체 무슨 말을 하는지 몰라서 선생님이 하는 말 마다
전자사전을 꺼내서 뜻을 해석하곤 했었다. 나는 한국에
서부터 말을 잘 안하고 묵묵히 들어주는 성격이었는데,
여기에 와서는 그러면 안된다는 것을 깨달았다. 내 무뚝
뚝한 얼굴이 선생님과 다른 ESL 아이들에게 많은 오해

를 불러 일으켰다. 내가 내 쌍둥이보다도 말수가 적어서
선생님은 내가 영어를 더 못하는 줄 알고 반 년간은 내
쌍둥이보다 더 낮은 수준의 ESL 듣도록 했었다. 그리고
ESL 선생에게서 의사에게 찾아가 보라는 말까지 들을
정도였다. ESL 선생님에게 받은 상처는 말로 할 수 없을
만큼, 지금까지 잊혀지지 않을만큼 큰 아픔으로 다가왔
었다.

힘들었던 9학년 생활을 마치고 나서 어쩔 수없이
이사때문에 학교를 Langley High School로 옮기게 되었
다. 이 학교에 와서는 더 많은 친구들을 사귀었었다. 하
지만 여전히 수업을 따라가기엔 벅찼다. 9학년 때 ESL
때문에 과학과목을 못듣고 9학년이 들어야 할 Biology
를 10학년 때 듣게 되었는데, 한국에서 내가 가장 자신
있어한 과목이 너무나도 내겐 벅차고 힘들었다. 매일
시험이 있을때 마다 밤을 새워가며 사전을 붙잡고 공부
하던 기억이 있다. 그리고 언어로 인한 오해때문에 웃지
못할 해프닝도 여러번 있었다. 지금은 웃을 수 있지만
그 일들로 인해서 엄마와 함께 얼마나 울었는지 모른다.

그렇게 버지니아에서 힘든 생활을 하다가, 아빠
가 또다시 뉴욕 본사로 발령이 나면서 우리는 뉴저지로
이사왔다. 뉴저지에 와서 훨씬 숨통이 트이는 느낌이었
다. 학교공부가 버지니아에서 공부했던것 보다 훨씬 쉽
고 즐거웠다. 그리고 여기에 와서 느꼈던 것은 나의 영
어실력과 성적이 해가 갈수록 점차 나아지고 것이었다.
그리고 이전에는 알지 못했지만 나의 성격도 점차 바뀌
고 있었다. 예전에는 낯선것만 보면 무조건 적대시 했었
지만 지금은 소극적으로나마 먼저 다가갈 줄 아는 사람
이 되었다. 그리고 또한 나처럼 무뚝뚝하고 말없는 친구

들을 보게되면 과거에 나를 보는것 같아 먼저 말 걸게되는 또한 그들의 냉정한 대답조차도 이해할 수 있다는 나를 보며 가끔 자랑스럽고 내 스스로 기특하다는 생각조차 하게된다.

내가 이렇게 성격이 바뀌게 된 것은 나의 느리고 고집센 모습들을 기다려주고 칭찬을 아끼지 않은 선생님들이 있었다는 것을 인정하지 않을수 없다. 나의 작은 일에도 칭찬과 격려로 나를 더 분발할 수 있게 해 주셨던 그 분들의 사랑을 나도 친구들과 다른 사람들에게 베풀고 싶다. 또한 늦게 열매맺어도 박수쳐 주고 고난을 이겨내고 승리한 것에 더 값진 박수를 쳐주는 이 미국이라는 나라에 나는 빚을 진 것 같다. 내 꿈은 앞으로 의사가 되고싶다. 환자와 아픔을 같이하고 먼저 말 걸어주고 화를 내도 참아줄 수 있는 그런 의사가 되고싶다. 더 나아가서 아프리카와 같은 제 3세계로 의료선교를 떠나 의료혜택을 받지 못하는 나라의 사람들을 치료해주고 싶다. 지금은 부족할지 모르지만 천천히 그 꿈을 향해 나아갈 것이다.

대화에 자신이 없었던 나. 언어에 자신이 없었던 나. 다른 사람들에게 성격적으로 문제가 있다고 여겨졌던 나. 쉽게 좌절했던 나. 사람들에게 냉정한 표정으로 주변을 힘들게 했던 내가 지금은 먼저 말걸고 주변을 웃음으로 변화시킬 수 있는 내가 되었는데 미래에 나는 얼마나 더 사람들에게 기쁨을 줄 수 있는 사람이 되어있을까. 내 부모님은 내가 나쁜 상황에 빠져 좌절하고 낙심했을 때, 이 일로 인해서 니가 인생이 끝난다면 하나님께서 미국에 가게해 달라고 했던 기도에 응답하지 않으셨다고 단호히 말씀하셨다. 내 인생은 하나님의 계획 가

운데 어떤 한 지점을 지나고 있는 중이라고 말씀하신다.
올라갈 때도 있고 내려갈 때도 있고, 하지만 나는 하나
님이 정해주신 목적을 향해 나아가는 중이라고.

　　　나는 믿는다. 이 말에 뜻이 가슴에 깊이 와닿지는
않지만 어렴풋이 그 의미가 나를 이끌고 있음을.

THE EXPERIENCE

Jinwoo Shim

On July 13th in 1991, I was born in a hospital in Seoul, a capital city of Korea. My mother says that it took 8 hours for her to give birth to me. I was relatively big compared to other babies. 7 months after I was born, my family went to England because of my dad's business. He was working for LG Company, and he was ordered to work in England for 5 years.

I can't remember precisely when I was in England probably because I was so young at that time. We used to live in New Malden, and I went to Westbury House School. Even though I barely remember some of my friend's faces, I have completely forgotten their names. Only one person I can remember is a boy named John. He was smaller than me, and he was living next to my house. Everyday, we met together and played together either on his house, or my house. I remember that one day, John and I were imitating the actions of Power Rangers broadcasting on TV. We also played a Super Mario game through my Nintendo game console. One thing I particularly remember about him is that he couldn't read anything so that I had taught him some alphabets. Anyway, he was my best friend in England and even though he had already forgotten me, I really want to see him again.

My parents say that when I was a baby, they took me and traveled around more than 15 countries. Although I don't remember most of them, I certainly remember when we went to the Euro Disney Land in France. There were many people riding ponies. My father and I also rode a pony together, and we controlled him to walk. However, instead of stepping his feet, the pony started to poop, and he did not stop it. He was basically walking while pooping continuously. Everyone was looking at our pony and was laughing at him.

When I was 5 years old, we came back to Korea. Because I just came back to Korea from England, I was more comfortable speaking English than Korean. However, I went to the Hanyang Kindergarten right away. My mom says that when I was young, one day, after I returned from my Kindergarten, I cursed at my mom. I did not know the meaning of what I was saying, and I was just imitating what my friends did. My mom was surprised and she immediately yelled at me.

When I was 7 years old, I started to attend Seohyun Elementary school. During my first year in the Seohyun Elementary School, I earned the nickname "Tiger" because I was the tallest person in the class. One day, when I was in the third grade, my mom gave me money and ordered me to go buy a tofu. While I was going to a supermarket, I saw people gathered around in a video arcade. I was interested at what was going on, so I went in there. There were also some of my friends playing the games. They were playing the game named Tekken, which is a 3D fighting game franchise released by Namco Company. Because I loved so much playing Tekken, instead of buying a tofu, I spent all my money playing games. When I came back to the house, I was scolded by my mom violently.

In 2002, when I was in fifth grade, there was a world cup being held in Korea and Japan. Amazingly, Korea had placed 4th in the world cup. Whenever there was a game, my family went outside and cheered Korea team just like other people did. Sometimes, I went out with my friends and went to a park, watching the game through a big screen. It was pretty funny that every one's mind was unified as one when cheering for the Korea team.

When I was 13 years old, I started to attend Seohyun Middle School. As I became a middle school student, I was gradually pressured by my grades. My grade was a little bit above the average. Although my parents wanted me to get better grades, I could never fulfill their desires. Instead, I liked playing with my friends a lot. After school, we would play soccer or go to internet café and play games. Also, sometimes, we went to karaoke and sang together.

The turning point in my life was the day that I learned I was moving to America. I was 14 years old, and just like normal students studying for tests, I was preparing for the final exam. While I was studying for science in my room right after I returned from my school, my mom came to me and said, "We are moving to America". At first, I didn't believe her, but her face was so solemn that I realized that she was not joking. She said that because my father is to be sent to America for his business trip, we have to follow him and stay in America for at least 3 years. I couldn't imagine myself being in America, which I heard and saw only through TV and books. I wasn't excited at all. I was rather shocked. As soon as I was convinced that we were truly moving to America, I threw out all my school stuff to the corner of my room.

I played computer games in the evening, and at night I went out to borrow 24 comic books. I called my friends, who were studying, through my cell phone. Their replies were brusque since they were nervous about the final exam which was about 1 week left. I said, "Hey! I'm moving to America!" They thought I was joking at first, but they eventually realized the seriousness of my words when I said "I don't have to study for the exam". "What the…?" they started to ask me several questions, but I just said "We can talk later, just pay attention to your work. I'll just read comic books. Bye". When I finished informing my friends, I was so happy not by the fact that I was moving to America, but by the fact that I didn't have to study for the exam.

Next day, when I went to the school, my classmates came to me and asked many questions. They were jealous of me because I didn't have to take the final exam. Because I learned that I was moving to America, I couldn't concentrate on my teacher's lessons. All of my teachers were astonished when I said I was moving to America. Interestingly, most of their responses were, "Wow, this class now would be less noisy". Although I was happy and was ready to be the noisiest person in the class, I didn't cause any trouble since I cared about my friends who will be taking the final exam. One week passed by very quickly, and it was the day of the final exams.

The test days were divided in 4 days. I didn't go to the school for the first 3 days. I just dawdled in my house, playing games, reading books, and watching movies. When it was the last day of the final exam, I went to the school. However, I didn't enter any classroom. Instead, I was outside of the school on the playground, kicking balls around and waiting for my friends to finish their exams. Since the playground was right in front of the school, if anyone sees outside the window, he would see me playing soccer alone. A dead silence was surrounding the school, and I could feel the intensity of students' concentration. I didn't make any noise and I was planning what I and my friends would do after the exam is over. Suddenly, I could hear someone saying "Hey!" I turned around and there was the principal of the school.

"What are you doing here?" asked the principal. He was thinking that I was one of the disorderly students of the school. In order to avoid a situation in which I have to explain to the principal for a long time, I answered differently from what my answer should have been. I replied to him that I was from another school and that I was waiting for my friends. He looked at me suspiciously for a while, but he eventually nodded his hair and went back to his office. This was the first time of my life talking to the principal of the school. As soon as the exam was over, I could meet my friends, and we enjoyed the freedom of burden.

Although I told my friends that I would leave several days after the exam – and I thought it was right – our estimated time of departure kept delaying. It delayed for almost 2 months. Consequently, I didn't have to study much during that time. However, I kept focusing on learning English since I couldn't just play around for 2 months. Ironically, because my departure was kept delaying, I had several farewell parties. As the time passes, my friends and even my teachers were asking "When are you leaving?" Finally, on June 23th, 2006, I took the plane going to America.

Before I describe my story in America, I want to introduce my family. I have a father, a mother and a younger sister.

My dad's name is Choonshik Shim, and after he worked for LG for a long time, he was recruited by Korea Provincial (State) Government to be a public servant. He grew up in a country side in Korea. According to my grandparents, my father used to study really hard. However, because my grand parents were very poor at that time, with 6 children including my dad, he had to help his parents' farm works during his school life. He couldn't have brand new clothes when his friends were wearing them. He couldn't eat properly, when his friends were eating delicious food. He even couldn't buy a single study-aid book when his friends were having tutors. My dad tenaciously studied hard, believing that he would achieve success later. When he graduated from his high school, he could enter one of the best universities in Korea. However, because my grandparents didn't have enough money to support him, my dad had to give up his plan and go to a less famous university to get tuition free. My grandparents say that he cried every night during that time. Later, while our family lived in England, my dad received MBA in London to get better educational background.

Because he used to study very well, his expectations on me are very high. He wants me to study well and go to a good university. He says that in order to prevent the sadness in which he suffered because of the lack of money, he would send me to a good university, if I get accepted, even though we would have to sell our house. Since I am the first son of the family, he is generally stricter with me than he is with my younger sister. When, for example, I and my sister are fighting, I would be the person to be blamed. In fact, if he gets angry, he is unstoppable. Also, his decision is so determined that one cannot object to his opinion. Nevertheless, he is my greatest teacher regarding morality. He taught me that I should always try to help others and consider the etiquette no matter what happens. His motto is: "Strict to oneself, generous to others." Furthermore, my father is a devoted son to my grandparents. Whenever I look at his attitude toward grandparents, I promise myself that I would be like him. Anyway, I like my dad, and I am truly sorry to him since I frequently couldn't satisfy his expectations.

If my dad is characterized as rough, softness would be the right quality to describe my mom. My mom's name is Hwisook Cho. She majored in Japanese language in university. After graduation, she worked for a long time in Mitsubishi Corporation, which is one of the biggest companies in Japan. She always keeps the house clean, and she cooks very well. She doesn't get angry often, and she takes care of me most of the time. For instance, when I am scolded by my dad for any reason, after my dad is gone, she would come to me and try to relieve the tension and encourage me. In fact, she is a fervent Christian, and she always prays for my future. She also laughs a lot when I joke. She never stops worrying about me. She would, for example, give me fruits every night to support my health for studying. As her actions illustrate, she has lots of tears.

She sympathizes with everything, even though I think it is a trivial matter. She also often cries at sad movies when no one is crying.

Strangely, my mom has an unbelievable power of recognizing my emotional mood. If I don't feel well, she would come to me and discuss the problem. Also, even though she doesn't say anything, if we go shopping, she would sometimes buy few of clothes, and let me buy many clothes in order to make me happy since I am distressed by my grades. I appreciate my mom's caring, and I am definitely going to be a dutiful son to my dad and my mom.

Also, my younger sister's name is Yoosun Shim, and she is 3 years younger than me. Interestingly, she has a citizenship of England because she was born there when I was in England. I would say that my sister is very capricious. Her behavior is always determined by her emotions at that time. If she is happy, for instance, if I order her to bring a cup of water, she would bring it to me immediately. On the other hand, if she is irritated, she would curse at me when I order her something to do.

Although we do fight a lot like other brothers and sisters, I can't imagine being the only child in our family. Because of her, I do not feel lonely every time. For example, if our family goes on a trip, it is obviously more fun to play with her, rather than being alone. Because she is a teenager, she knows the idol singers or actors I like. We would discuss some new songs and talk about the TV shows. Since we share common characteristics as teenagers, I can talk to her about things that my parents probably wouldn't understand.

Although it is not a human, I regard one more as our family. It is a dog named "Janggoon," which means "General" in English. He is a Maltiz which has white furs. In fact, my dad didn't like raising dogs. After I and my sister persuaded him for a long time, we bought Janggoon when it was only 2 months after his birth. We raised him for 3 years, and we did have lots of fond memories with him. Whenever we traveled or went hiking, we brought him with us. Because he flattered a lot, he was like vitamin, which made us lively. As his name suggests, he was a belligerent one, and we always had to stop him trying to fight huge dogs. Indeed, it was a tragic disaster when we learned that we couldn't bring him to America, since the owner of the house, where we would live in America, stated that no pets were allowed. We had to leave Janggoon in my grandparent's house, making us long for the day we would return to Korea.

The flight from Korea to U.S. almost took 13 hours. When I arrived at John F. Kennedy airport in New York, I was overwhelmed by the fact that I was in a different country. My heart began to pound as I saw foreigners around me. Every signboard was written in English, and I could hear people talking to each other although I couldn't translate their words. When we came out of the airport, it was night, and we were heading to my dad's friend's house. Amazingly, our family and my dad's friend's family had met in England when I was living there. Although I didn't remember, my mom said that I used to play well with Sunghoon Lim, my dad's friend's son. Anyway, we went to Sunghoon's house, and had dinner together. It was truly awkward when I first saw Sunghoon because I really couldn't remember who he was. However, we soon got along together when we played games together. Without knowing anyone in America, Sunghoon became my first, and the best friend.

I went to Tenafly High School since the school was known for its good education. Sunghoon was also going there since he had just graduated from Tenafly Middle School. When I was in Korea, I thought that if I go to America, I would be surrounded by Americans. However, my prediction was a total mistake. Interestingly, there were many Koreans in the high school. Later, I learned that there are many Koreans in New Jersey, a state where I live. I really want to thank Sunghoon using this opportunity because I was able to make many good friends, like Seunghoon Han, Seongwon Jeon, and Jahyuk Lee whom Lloyd introduced to me.

The first obstacle I had to face when I came to America was the language problem. What I learned from Korea did not help me at all, and I had to study English really hard. Students from foreign countries were to take ELL (English Language Learners) test. If they pass the test, they can take regular English class, but if they don't, they would take ELL class in which on-English speaking students are attending. ELL class was divided into three classes, beginner, intermediate, and advanced. I took the ELL test, and I was placed in ELL Advance class. People, including my friends, were surprised at my ELL test result because most students who just came from foreign countries went to ELL beginner class or intermediate class. Ironically, because I got into ELL Advance class, they thought that I was receiving good grades in Korea when I was really not.

The major issue among ELL class students was *who can pass the ELL test really fast?* The average time of ELL students to pass ELL test was about three years. Many of ELL students, including me, envied my friend, Esther, who passed ELL in one and a half year. I was very eager to know how she passed ELL test fast, so I asked her. She replied, "Well, I just tried to imitate the speaking styles of my American friends. That's it. If you keep doing that, you may also learn vocabularies even though you did not study them." I became speechless. After the day I listened to Esther, I followed the same path blindly which Esther had taken before. I watched Disney channels, trying to watch them without subtitles, listened to pop music, and joined soccer team where I could speak to Americans. I could feel that, day by day, my English ability was gradually increasing.

It is hard not to mention my ELL teachers when talking about my improved English. Mrs. Eliscu, Mrs. Derdemezis, and Ms. Edelman were my ELL advanced teachers, and their lessons helped me a lot. In Mrs. Eliscu's class, she would cover parts of grammar and vocabulary. In

Mrs. D's class, we mainly focused on Literature such as <u>Of Mice and Men</u>, and <u>Jane Eyre</u>. In Ms. Edelman's class, we practiced writing paragraphs and essays. All of those lessons significantly impacted my English, and I was able to pass ELL in one year.

When I was a sophomore, I could enroll in regular classes. However, although I had passed ELL, I still had language problems because I didn't perfectly master English. Even though I could mostly understand what teachers were saying, I sometimes couldn't understand what my American friends were saying, probably because they were talking fast. This made me to talk not often to American friends because I was afraid of the possibility that I would misunderstand their what they were saying. My negative thinking, nevertheless, was transformed by one significant event.

During my 10th grade, I was taking a biology class. One day, Ms. Halliwell, my biology teacher, announced that there will be a project consisted of Paper work and Presentation. The topic of the project was Human Genetic Disorders, and each person had to hand in his paper works and present his research work in front of the classmates. I could hear some sighs among students, but I couldn't even sigh. Her words struck me, and I soon became chaotic. I did have some projects in other regular classes, but those were group projects so I could just memorize and say my lines, which were generally short because of my lack of English speaking ability. Despite my state of disorderliness, Ms. Halliwell continued to explain how the project is going to be and how it will be graded. What she said was that the project will be total of 100 points, in which the paper work is 50 points, and the presentation is 50 points. When doing a presentation, each person would come out and present his work in 3-5 minutes. This was my first project to present my work in regular class all by myself. Anyway, in front of the classroom, there were many sticks in a bottle, and each person had to pick one stick randomly. Each name of the diseases was written on each stick so that a person had to research whatever was written on his stick. When I picked my stick, I could see *Amyotrophic Lateral Sclerosis* written on it. I was frustrated because it was so hard to pronounce it.

After the school, I researched about what my assigned disease was, and I could find out that *Amyotrophic Lateral Sclerosis* was, in fact, another name of Lou Gehrig's disease. I had to research many things about Lou Gehrig's disease. There were 7 questions in total, but I had to spend much time in answering one question. For example, one question would be like, "What are the symptoms of the disorder? Include the characteristics of an individual with the disorder, the affects of the disorder on the individual, and the phenotypes of the disorder". In general, I had to find out about the symptoms, how to detect the disease, the target of the disease, the inheritance pattern of the disease, life expectancy for one with the disorder, and the treatment options for a patient. I researched them rigorously, thinking that I had to get perfect score on the paper work because I would get low points on the presentation. I spend lots of times working on the paperwork, and I could finish the work earlier than my friends did.

The grading of the presentation was divided into 5 parts, including preparedness, eye contact, visual, content, and time-limit. I first summarized important facts from my paper work and then read it for practice. When I timed my speech, it came out to be around 4 minutes and 30 seconds. For most of the people, 4 minutes and 30 seconds would be seen as a very short time. However, if a person actually times himself and tries to speak continuously for that amount of time, he will easily discover that it is a pretty long time for the speaker. Basically, I practiced and practiced. I asked my friends to pronounce all the words that I wasn't sure how to do it. As a result of my practice, I could almost memorize everything written on my research paper. Indeed, I did not want to be embarrassed in front of my friends.

Eventually, the project day came. Even though I was relieved because I had practiced a lot, as my classmates finished their presentations, one by one, my heart began to pound hastily. And then, it was my turn. I went out to the front of the class, attached my visual show work on the blackboard, and began to speak. When I raised my voice and began to speak, I suddenly lost all my confidence, and I could discover myself keep looking at the flash cards. I could feel my back starting to produce sweat. However, as the time passed, when I was saying, I could remember what my next line would be. Line by line crossed my mind, and I gradually regained my confidence of my practice. I rarely looked at my flash cards, and just talked about what popped into my mind. The 4 minute and 30 seconds went by instantly, and I was somehow so proud at myself when I finished my presentation. Even though my classmates clapped when everyone finished his presentation, when it was my turn to receive such claps, I was euphoric.

After the day of the presentation, one day, we received our grades of the project. I was shocked to see my grade because it was 100%. Friends surrounding me were also shocked at my grade, and they began to congratulate me. I forgot all about my hardships regarding preparing for the project, and I was certainly satisfied by the reward. I could again hear some sighs among my friends, and this time again, I couldn't sigh. I was so elated.

This small event would be indifferent to many others, but for me, it encouraged me a lot. It proved the point that if one actually tries hard, he can conquer the problem despite the disadvantages. In my case, I, who couldn't speak English fluently, received better grades than most of my friends born in America. Since the biology project, whenever there was another project in other classes, I was, at least, not afraid of it.

Besides my high school, another – more different setting – has occupied my high school life; namely, my volunteer service. It's a different world, but a very special world to me, nonetheless.

"You like me?" Howard would shout to Nicole as usual, smiling happily. Nicole would reply "No! I like Justin!" basically ignoring Howard. Then I would hear Howard murmuring "Why...? Why..?" This conversation is what I hear every Monday afternoon after school. I have been volunteering in a place called Milal ever since November, 2007. Howard openly loves Nicole, but Nicole has loved her school classmate Justin for more than 2 years. Howard tries to take care of Nicole in everyway, like bringing a cup of water for Nicole after dinner or giving his clothes when Nicole is shivering. Although Howard doesn't know most of the alphabets, he can write "Nicole" easily.

4:30 p.m. is the time for them to study alphabets. "Okay, now let's study guys" I would say. Both Howard and Nicole are pretty old to learn alphabets since they are over 15 years old. Although it had been more than a year that I taught them alphabets, they still have not mastered the alphabets.

Nicole is really amazing at puzzles. Her hobby is to play puzzles, and she plays it everyday. She doesn't need any instruction. In fact, people need instructions from her. I had once competed with Nicole, and I completely lost to her. There are also other handicapped members in Milal. Seoyong, who is over 30 years old, likes me, and she always says "cute" to me. She really likes the word "beautiful" so I would always try to use that word for her. For example, if she is wearing a new hat, I would say "your hat is beautiful". She would laugh incessantly. There are also Jieun, Dayung, and Susan. Jieun is the person who has the most laughter in Milal. She would laugh aloud at something even though it really wasn't funny. When she begins to laugh, it is hard to stop her laughing. Dayung is the cleverest person among the handicapped people in Milal. She knows many words and can write them even though she is the youngest of all. Because she is good at folding papers into various figures, we learn some folding skills from her such as folding papers into frogs or ships. Lastly, Susan is the quietest one in Milal. Most of the time, she is looking at windows, holding a thread. The reason that she is holding a thread is that she loves untying tangled thread. No matter how the thread is tangled complicatedly, she can untie it. Whenever I tangle the thread for her, believing that this time she cannot untie this, every time I end up being frustrated by her skill.

Indeed, frankly, at first, I did start this volunteering just for the volunteer activity which I would turn in to get into a good college I aspired to. However, as time passed, I got very familiar with everyone at Milal, seeing them after school on Monday that I actually began to enjoy spending time with them. Because I know each person's characteristics very well, I would advise a newly volunteering person coming on Monday. My special ties to Milal friends made me familiar with handicapped people, and I really appreciate that. What I learned from my Milal activity is that handicapped people are pure. Nowadays, the world is filled with many bad people who commit crimes indifferently. Even though those people are healthy, they use their advantageous bodies for bad purposes.

What I also want to mention is that handicapped people need attention. Numerous people tend to avoid handicapped people, ignoring them when they need help. From my Milal activity, I realized that caring would make handicapped people happy. Even a small care, like talking to them, makes them happy. Whenever I look at my Milal friends and see their bright smiles, I do hope that people, who have bad prejudiced opinions against handicapped people, would actually try to help them even though they are not forced to do so.

After Milal, I became enamored of volunteerism. Although I could not wrest too much time away from my studies, since college applications were right around the corner, I tried to get involved with volunteer activities, whenever I could. I enjoyed helping people; and I learned a lot from the people I served.

The most memorable day in my life occurred during the summer vacation in 2009, when I went to the camp, called "Wildlife Experience". The Wildlife Experience Summer Program was the 7-day program which offered the youth the opportunity to learn to value their lives through daily community service activities. I did not intend to go to this camp because I have never experienced camping, and since I was turning into a high school senior, I thought studying for the SAT was the most crucial part at that time. However, I was encouraged to go to the program because of my dad, who was lured by a Columbian college student whom I even don't know. My dad was saying that the student who got accepted to Columbia College recommended this program so that I should go there. Since I did not want to defy my father and thinking that I might help some people in need, I decided to go there, not knowing that I would meet a person whom I would never forget in my life.

As I had expected, the condition of the camping site was hard to endure. About 60 people joined the program; about 40 people were males and 20 people were females. Despite our numbers, however, there was only one washbasin and one toilet. The toilet was extremely dirty, and there were many bugs crawling around inside the toilet. As a result, many boys happened to urinate secretly on the bush. Also, the funny thing is that if one wants to brush his teeth, he would be in a line of 60 people since there was one old washbasin. The most horrible thing about the camping site was that there was no shower room. We had to ride a van for about 5 minutes and go to a shower room on the seaside. In fact, we could take showers once in 2~3 days. Unfortunately, even if we go to the shower room, only two people could shower at a time, so the last person had to wait more than one hour to take a shower. These conditions of the camping site shocked me, and I really desired to go back home and take a hot bath.

Despite all the bad situations, the camp was not as bad as I thought. I could meet many good friends, especially my group mates. Our group consisted of 6 people including Jason, Brian, David, Jonny, Kyung, and me. Jonny was our group leader and we created our group's name as Goonies, which meant "real men" according to Jonny. Everyday, we had to sleep in a relatively small tent compared to our body sizes. The tent was very messy because although Brian, Kyung, and I cleaned our stuffs every time, Jonny, David, and Jason did not arrange their clothes, sleeping bags, and even trash in order. The schedule for every day was simple. We would wake up at 6:30 a.m., and eat breakfast which was always bagels with cereals. After the breakfast, we would go to our assigned missions which were different every day. The missions usually took about 5 hours and the time we returned to our camps would be 5:00 p.m. There were no books, computers, or TVs in the camping site so we had to kill our time by playing "Killer Ball".

"Killer Ball" was a game that required one valley ball and at least 6 people to have fun. People would make a circle and start passing the ball to each other. If one tosses the ball in a wrong way, or fails to toss back the ball coming toward him properly, he would go to the middle of the circle. As soon as there is at least one person in the middle of the circle, surrounding people can smash the middle one with the ball while they are passing the ball around. This simple game was the most popular activity among us. Every time, more than 20 people played the game, and we could enjoy ourselves.

After playing "Killer Ball", we would eat dinner around 7:00 p.m., and after dinner, we would again have free time until 11:00 p.m. and go to our tents. However, we would not sleep as soon as we go back to our tents and lie down. In my case, our group mates shared nasty, nostalgic, funny, scary, even embarrassing stories. It really was a good time, and I extremely like it. Our friendships grew stronger as we made jokes and laughed together.

There were 5 missions in Wildlife Experience Summer Program. We had no choice, but to go to Buckingham Nursing Home, Newark Rescue Mission, NYC Rescue Mission, Westchester Habitat for Humanity, and Sullivan Correctional Facility. Briefly, in Buckingham Nursing Home, we had to prepare for the talent shows. Everyone had to participate in the talent show somehow so I just danced with my friends using the song "Closer" while others sang or played instruments. Our purpose for talent shows was to entertain old people in the Nursing Home. Fortunately, they enjoyed our shows, and some even showed their tears since we reminded them of their grandparents. In Westchester Habitat for Humanity, we had to help building the house for homeless people. In my case, I had to remove lots of heavy stones that were in the way of constructing a house. I even had to saw the branches of trees that were over the fence and were leaning toward the house. In Sullivan Correctional Facility, we would listen to testimonies of prisoners who regretted what they had done. They enthusiastically appealed to us not to be like them and make a bad decision. Their sincere testimonies were indeed unforgettable.

The most memorable day in my life was the third day of my camping when I went to NYC Rescue Mission. We went to Chinatown and arrived at our destination. Our destination was the building that was based on Christianity, and it was the free home for homeless people in New York City. The volunteers, including me, were divided into several groups to help out the people in the building. My job was to wash every window on the first floor with my friend Matt. Even climbing a ladder, we washed all the windows cautiously using a patch and a Windex, a cleaning tool. We also had to rearrange all the chairs in the auditorium and wash every single one of them. After all the work, Matt went to the bathroom, and I was resting on the chair in the auditorium.

"Where are you from?" I looked back, and there was an African American sitting behind next to me. He looked tough, since he had a scar on his face, and he was muscular. I politely replied that I was from Korea. He asked my name and we soon started to talk to each other and I could learn a lot about him.

He was 26 years old. He never saw his mother, and he was in a prison for more than 6 years. He had committed many sins, such as raping, cheating on his girlfriend, doing drugs, and shooting a person. I was fascinated by his life story, and I could see myself feeling sorry for him. Suddenly, he asked me "Do you believe in God?" I was embarrassed to say that I believe in God because although I was going to a church, I was kind of forced to go there by my mom. I answered him frankly that I do not believe in God since there are some God's words that I can't understand. For example, I heard that any person who doesn't believe in God is going to hell. I was wondering about a person, who didn't have a chance to know about God. I thought that in that case, if the person goes to hell, God is being unfair. When I asked him about this question, he answered "Yeah, I did think about that problem for a long time. For example, there are many people in Africa, and many of them certainly don't have the chance to know about God. However, if they look around themselves, they can see rocks, trees, and animals. Right? If they think that there is some kind of God who created such things, they can go to heaven." I could grasp what he was saying, and I was surprised at his faith in God. I asked him more questions about God, and he answered every thing. After all the questioning, he said that I should believe in God and that he would pray for me. We prayed together for a long time. After the praying it was time for me to leave the place and go back to the camp. When all the volunteers had gathered and were ready to leave, the African American, who prayed for me, came to me and gave me a cross. The cross had a color of copper, and it was extremely worn down. He said, "Jin, this cross is very precious to me. I always carried this cross since I started to believe in God. I'll give this cross to you. I really hope, one day, you would sincerely believe in God." Every volunteer clapped and cheered, and I was moved by his words and actions.

I couldn't find out his name because he refused to tell his name to me. However, he was the first American whom I talked with more than 2 hours. Since I came to America, I met many good teachers and friends, but none of them was comparable to him. That 2 hours of talking really got into my heart, and I strongly want to meet him again. After meeting him, I could discover myself paying attention to my pastor's words more enthusiastically than I did before, and I was happy to go to the church. I hope he would read this book and remember me. Through this book, I want to say to him that I always carry the cross he gave to me.

TWIN PIANIST

Haein Lee

There is this girl I know really well that I think you might like. She's funny and outgoing, but also prudent. It is easy to get to know her if you just give it a chance. Who do you ask? I'm talking about myself, Haein Lee.

There were many ups and downs before I was born. My mother got pregnant when my older sister was 3 years old. She recognized that we were twins and girls, 8 months after the pregnancy. At the time I was born, there was still boy-preferring culture in Korea, so my mother would have been treated badly by others because she would have only 3 daughters and no sons. One of the doctors, who told mother that we are twin girls, even recommended an abortion. However, since my mother told people that we are twins, they started waiting for me and my twin sister.

On October 28, 1991, in Seoul, I and my twin sister were born healthy at 6 pound. But my mother always thought that we were too skinny, compared to my older sister. Even though I came out only 1 minute ahead of my sister, my father gave me a name, Haein, which means, "A generous person as sea." I was called "Haein" after a famous poetess in Korea.

No one ever was like my grandparents who were glad to see me and my sister. To be honest, my grandmother did not expect us because she loved my older sister too much. Later, my grandmother told me when I became an elementary school student, that she "fell in love" right after she met us. My twin sister and I spent time with grandparents, every half a year. My mother got disappointed to be far apart from us, but also felt bitter because we seemed like we liked my grandparents more than mother and father.

When I became 2, our family left Korea because of father's business, for 3 years. We had the happiest and the most plentiful moments in Hong Kong. I had all the advantages in life, such as barbequing with church friends during the weekend, going to the swimming pool, almost every day, and going to tourist attractions in Hon Kong, which I couldn't have done in Korea. Furthermore, I and my twin sister always gained other's affections wherever I went. The other day, I stole a glance into my father's diary. It said that my father's happiest moment in his life was the life in Hong Kong. I was very surprised but empathized.

3 years after the blessed moments in Hong Kong, we went back to Korea. My Korean was really bad because I did not go to a Korean kindergarten in Hong Kong. I even still remember that some children teased me because of my poor Korean. I was under pressure as I faced the problem of language. And then, one day, I caught a disease called, Facial Paralysis. I got better quickly, but my health gradually failed. As I was in failing health, I lost my confidence. I also couldn't get along with the Korean schools system. I think that it is because my lifestyle was very different from common Korean kids'. I got stressed again when I went to middle school. Strict rules and teachers, a heavy atmosphere, and the reality of a competitive spirit between students were very unfamiliar to me. Eventually, my grades fell down.

I became sick again when I was 13 years old. I was really shocked and everything in my life seemed to be ruined. My body became weaker and weaker, and I couldn't do anything completely by myself, resulting in infinite tiredness. People around me started to sympathize with me, and I became a spoilt dependent child.

However, I could endure hard time with my friends, by spending happy times. We always hung out together after we finished school exams. One of the happiest memories with my friends was that we built a house with caramels and chocolates, tried to imitate a house of sweets from the story called, "Hensel and Gretel", on Christmas Eve. This memory still makes me smile. We also shared sticker photos before I came to America. I still can't forget that my friends sent me and my twin sister presents from Korea on my first birthday in the United States. Even though we haven't contact each other since long time ago because we all are preparing for college, I think we will always be great friends as 3 years ago.

The first time I came in touch with piano was when I saw my mom playing piano for the first time in my life, when I was 7. Since then, I was eager to play piano. When someone asked about my future dream, I always answered 'pianist'. I started getting down to prepare for a Music College, when I was first year in middle school. But after awhile, I became sick, and I had to stop playing piano again.

2 years after wasting time, when I became 9th grader, my father was posted overseas. It was 3 months before we came to America. I was studying for final exams at home when my father told me that we were going to the US for 3 years. After I heard what my father said, I felt like I could fly to the sky. I remember that I couldn't even sleep that night, dreaming about me speaking English fluently. We

arrived in America, in the State of Virginia, on August 26, 2006.

There is a Korean proverb, "Well begun is half done." But my first start in America didn't go that well. I couldn't speak any English out of my mouth, such as asking for the bathroom. I became ashamed of myself when people talked to me in English, and I couldn't answer. My first school in Virginia was ranked among top 10 public schools in the United States. Its atmosphere was also strict as schools in Korea. I think it was harder to keep good grades in American high schools than Korean high schools. My body couldn't stand this situation so I was always sick, and I constantly suffered because of English problems. What made matters worse was that we had a car accident. When my mom drove my twin sister and me to school on one winter morning, someone crashed our car. Because of the car accident, we had to go to court and this situation made us suffer more. On second thought, I think I feared to adapt to new circumstances even though I faced day-to-day happenings.

While we had hard time in Virginia, my father relocated, so our family came to New Jersey. I felt like I could breathe easy in New Jersey. However, I soon felt like a loser because I still couldn't get good grades in a new school, even though I tried so hard. Meanwhile, I was operated on for rhinitis, and since then I became healthier, little by little. I started piano again, last year, and I think I have gained confidence after this. People encouraged me, and I finally decided to major in music. I also started a church pianist at my church in New Jersey. I became an outgoing person, as I befriended many church friends.

On August, 2009, my father suddenly had to go back to Korea. My older sister transferred to University in Maine. Now, my mother, twin sister and I are the only family members in our house. Although we were afraid about staying in America without father and sad, I resolved not to disappoint my parents, by studying hard.

I'm satisfied with myself, now. Before, I was just a mere child and always made an excuse for myself when I faced problems. Now, I am changed. Especially, while I started playing the piano, I gained confidence in myself when I noticed my piano skill becoming gradually better. Of course I know that I am still not good at piano as other people, but I believe that there's nothing impossible if I could be diligent. It's unbelievable that I now speak, read, and write in English. I am proud of myself.

My mother always tells me that God never sent me to America to let me down. Even though I'm insufficient now, I could be great after 10, 20 years later. And I'm also curious about my future.

나의 자서전
이해인

　　여기 한 소녀가 있다. 　활달해 보이면서도 과묵하고, 남과 어울리는 걸 좋아하는 것 같으면서도 혼자만의 시간을 원하는, 냉소적인 듯 보이지만 마음은 따뜻한 소녀. 바로 나, 이해인이다.

　　나는 태어나기 전부터 우여곡절이 많았다. 엄마는 언니를 낳은 지 3 년 만에 나와 내 쌍둥이 여동생을 가지셨는데, 임신 8 개월이 되어서야 우리가 쌍둥이라는 것을 알게 되셨다고 한다. 그 때 당시만 해도 한국에선 여자가 아들을 낳지 못하면 안 좋은 시선을 받곤 했다. 우리가 태어나면 엄마는 딸 셋의

어머니라는 불명예를 안게 되는 것이었다. 한 병원에서는 우리가 여자아이라는 사실을 엄마에게 알려주면서 낙태를 권하기까지 했다고 한다. 하지만 놀랍게도 엄마가 주위 사람들에게 우리가 쌍둥이라는 사실을 알리자 모두들 우리가 태어나기를 기다리기 시작했다.

그 모든 일을 뒤로 하고 1991 년 10 월 28 일. 나와 내 쌍둥이 동생은 키 49cm, 2.7kg 으로 건강하게 태어났다. 하지만 먼저 태어났던 언니에 비해 우리가 성에 차지 않는지 엄마는 우리를 늘 마르게 보셨다고 한다. 비록 1 분이지만 먼저 이 세상에 나온 나는 태어나자 마자 '해인'이라는 이름을 갖게 됐다. 바다처럼 넓고 깊은 아량을 가진 아이라는 뜻의 내 이름은 아빠가 내가 태어나자마자 지어주신 이름이다. 아빠가 평소에 좋아하셨던 시인 이해인 수녀의 이름을 따서 지으신 것이라고 한다.

우리가 태어나자 무엇보다 기뻐하셨던 건 바로 우리 외할머니였다. 할머니는 사실 먼저 태어난 언니를 너무 예뻐했기 때문에 우리가 태어나도 별로 예뻐하지 않으실 줄 알았는데, 우리를 보자마자 '사랑에 빠지셨다고' 훗날 말씀해 주셨다. 그렇게 나와 내 쌍둥이 동생은 매년마다 1 년의 반 이상을 외조부모님과 부산에서 보냈다. 엄마는 물론 우리와 떨어져 있는게 많이 섭섭했지만, 엄마와 떨어져도 별로 엄마를 찾지 않고 오히려 외조부모님을 더 좋아하는 우리의 태도에 많이 야속하기도 하셨다고 한다.

내가 만 2 살이 되던 해인 1994 년, 우리 가족은 아빠의 일 때문에 홍콩으로 3 년간 떠났다. 우리는 홍콩에서 그 누구보다도 행복하고 풍요로운 시간을 보냈던 것 같다. 주말에 교회 사람들과 바베큐 파티를 했던 일, 아파트 단지 내의 수영장을 거의 매일 출석하다시피 다녔던 일, 여러 홍콩의 관광 명소들을 우리집 앞마당처럼 다녔던 일 등등 한국에선 불가능 한, 그런 특권을 누렸었던 것 같다. 그리고 우리는 어딜가나 쌍둥이라는 이유로 사람들에게 사랑을 받았었다. 그렇게 우리 가족은 정말 즐겁고 행복한 시간을 보냈었다. 언젠가 아빠의 일기를 훔쳐 본 적이 있었는데, 아빠 인생 중에서 가장 행복했던 시간이 바로 홍콩에서 살던 시절이었다는 것에 놀라기도 했고, 공감이 갔다.

그렇게 행복한 3년이라는 시간을 홍콩에서 보낸 후, 우리는 다시 한국으로 돌아갔다. 홍콩에서의 행복은 잠깐, 우리는 언어 문제로 스트레스를 받기 시작했다. 홍콩에서 살 당시 유치원을 다니지 않았던 나의 한국어가 또래 애들보다 훨씬 서툴렀다고 한다. 그것 때문에 친구들과 문제가 있었던 모양인지 스트레스를 많이 받았다. 그러다가 구안와사라는 얼굴의 반이 마비되는 병에 걸리게 됐다. 어렸기 때문이었는지 다행이도 2주만에 낫긴 했지만, 그 이후로 늘 살이 찌지 않고 건강에 자신이 없어지면서 점차 성격이 내성적으로 변해갔다.

어렸을 때부터 또래 한국 아이들과는 다른 생활을 했던 모양인지 한국 학교의 체제가 나에게 맞지 않았었다. 초등학교는 그럭저럭 다닐 만 했지만, 중학교에 가서부터 또다시 스트레스를 받기 시작했다. 자유롭지 못한 수업과 공부만이 성공하는 유일한 길이라는 식으로 말씀하시는 선생님들, 그리고 친구들끼리 서로 경쟁하는 팽팽한 분위기가 무척 낯설게 다가왔다. 학교에서의 내 등수와 성적은 곤두박질 칠 수 밖에 없었다.

그 와중에 나는 또 다시 안면마비 증상이 나타났다. 이 안면마비는 나에게 큰 충격을 주었고 완벽하게 회복되지 않은 내 얼굴을 보면서 나는 심한 좌절감에 빠지게 되었다. 몸은 더욱 더 약해지고, 나는 늘 어지럼증과 피곤함이 나를 따라다니며 무엇을 해도 의욕이 생기지 않는 이런 몸 상태 때문에 공부든 피아노든 어떤 것을 해도 만족할 만한 결과가 나오지 않았다. 그래서 나는 사람들의 동정과 관심을 받으면서 점점 더 응석받이가 되어 버렸고, 나 혼자서는 아무것도 할 수 없을 정도로 의존적 성향이 강해져만 갔다. 중학교에 막 들어갈 때까지만 해도 내 쌍둥이인 다인이보다 성적이 좋았었지만, 가면 갈수록 무엇하나

다인이보다 잘 하는게 없어서 밖으로 내색은 안 했지만 내 나름대로 자존심에 상처를 입기도 했었다.

하지만 그런 힘든 상황 속에서도 나는 친구들과 함께 행복한 시간을 보냈다. 난 아직도 크리스마스 이브에 친구집에 모여 과자집을 만든 일, 시험이 끝날 때마다 늘 함께 놀러나갔 일, 스티커 사진을 찍었던 일 등의 즐거웠던 그때를 생각하면 힘들다가도 미소가 지어지곤 한다. 또래들보다 어른스러웠던 내 친구들은 유난히 철이 없었던 나를 변화시켜 줬던것 같다. 내가 미국에 와서 첫 번째 생일을 맞았을때, 국제 우편으로 선물과 편지를 보내준 것을 아직도 잊지 못한다. 물론 지금은 친구들도 대입 준비를 하느라 바빠서 연락을 못 하지만, 오랜만에 만나도 우리는 3 년전에 헤어졌던 그대로 어색하지 않을 것 같다.

내가 피아노를 처음으로 만난것은 7 살때 엄마의 피아노 연주를 본 것이었다. 그 때부터 피아노라는 악기에 푹 빠져들기 시작해서 엄마에게 피아노 학원에 보내달라고 졸랐고, 그 때부터 누군가가 나의 장래희망을 물어보면 나의 대답은 언제나 '피아니스트'였다. 여러가지 사정으로 하다가 말았다를 반복하다 본격적으로 피아노 전공을 준비하기 시작했던 건 중학교 1 학년때였다. 하지만 불행하게도 전공 준비를 시작한 지 얼마 지나지 않아서 두번째로 두번째 안면마비에 걸렸고, 또 다시 피아노를 그만둬야 했다.

그렇게 흐지부지 2 년이 지나 내가 중학교 3 학년이 됐을 무렵, 아빠가 주재원으로 발령이 나서 우리 가족은 미국에 오게 됐다. 미국에 오기 3 개월 전 중간고사를 위해서 공부하고 있을때 아빠가 퇴근하셔서 갑자기 우리가 미국으로 떠나게 되었다고 말씀하신 순간, 하늘을 날아갈 것 같았다. 3 년 후의 가장 자신없는 과목이었던 영어를 유창하게 하는 내 모습을 상상하면서 잠도 못 이뤘던 기억이 난다. 그렇게 한국에서의 모든 것을 뒤로하고 2006 년 8 월 26 일 아침, 우리는 미국 버지니아에 도착했다.

하지만 미국에서의 첫 출발은 그렇게 순탄치만은 못했다. 가장 기본적인 영어도 할 줄 몰라 학교 첫날에 쩔쩔맸던 일, 선생님의 말을 알아듣지 못해 내 자신이 바보로 느껴졌던 일 등등, 다시는 겪고 싶지 않은 부끄러운 일을 많이 겪었었다. 내가 미국에 처음 와서 다녔던 버지니아의 학교는 전국에서 10 등안에 들 정도로 수준이 높은 공립학교였다. 학교의 분위기는 한국 못지않게 엄격했었고, 오히려 큰 시험 한두번으로 성적을 올리는 한국에서보다 점수를 유지하기가 더 힘들었다. 언어 문제로 인해서 생긴 여러가지 스트레스와 약한 건강때문에 나는 늘 많이 아팠다. 엎친 데 덮친 격으로 교통사고까지 당하게 되었다. 눈이 오는 아침에 미끄러진 뒷차가 우리 차를 박은 것이었다. 그로 인해서 1년 동안 정신적 고통을 당하며 법정까지 가야 하는 등 힘든 상황 속에서 스트레스는 날로 쌓여만 갔다. 지금 생각해보면 미국이라는 사회에서 일어날 수 있는 일반적인 사건인데 새로운 일이 터질 때마다 새로운 상황과 부딪혀야 하는 것 때문에 더 많이 괴로워 했던 것 같다.

그렇게 버지니아에서 힘든 생활을 하다가, 아빠가 또다시 뉴욕 본사로 발령이 나면서 우리는 뉴저지로 이사왔다. 뉴저지에 와서 훨씬 숨통이 트이는 느낌이었다. 훨씬 자유로운 분위기의 학교와 선생님들이 좋았지만, 아무리 노력해도 내가 원하는 점수가 나오지 않아 늘 낙심했다. 그러던 중 나는 심각해진 비염 때문에 수술을 받게 되었는데, 나는 수술 후 몇 년 만에 처음으로 시원하게 숨쉬어 보는 감격을 맛보게 되었다. 이로 인해서 건강이 조금씩 회복되고 자신감을 회복하게 되었다. 성적이 잘 나오지 않아도 쉽게 낙심하지 않고 좀 더 긍정적인 생각을 하게 되었으며 작년부터 피아노를 다시 시작했는데, 피아노를 칠 때 마다 자신감을 얻는 것 같았다. 또한 주변의 부모님과 선생님들이 늦었지만 할 수 있다라고 나를 격려해 주신 것은 내가 피아노를 전공할 수 있다는 생각을 하게 했고, 정말 극적으로 2009년 1월에 다시 피아노 전공 준비를 시작했다. 전공 준비를 시작하면서 교회 반주도 시작했고, 서먹했던 교회 친구들과의 관계도 자연스럽게 좋아지기 시작했다.

그러던 중 2009년 8월에 아빠가 한국으로 다시 들어가셨다. 언니는 메인에 있는 학교로 편입하게 되었고, 엄마와 나 그리고 내 쌍둥이 다인이 이렇게 셋만이 남게 되었다. 처음엔 아빠와의 헤어짐 때문에 너무 두렵고 눈물도 많이 났지만 지금은 우리 때문에 한국에서 고생하시는 아빠를 위해서라도, 또 여기서 우리를 위해서 아빠와 떨어져 혼자 계신 엄마를 위해서라도 내가 더 열심히 공부해야 되겠다는 생각을 하며 내 마음을 다잡아갔다.

난 지금 내 모습에 만족한다. 예전에는 그저 아프다는 핑계로 모든 걸 미루는 철없는 어린아이였지만, 미국에 와서 여러가지 새로운 것들을 접하면서 내가 바뀌었다. 특히, 내가 좋아하는 피아노를 치기 시작하고 나날이 늘어가는 내 실력을 보면서 내성적이고 늘 새로운 것에 대해 부정적인 생각을 가졌던 나의 태도가 달라졌다. 늦게 전공을 준비해서 일찍 피아노를 시작한 다른 사람들에 비해선 아직은 턱없이 부족한 실력이지만, 늘 기도하면서 내가 하는 모든 일에 성실하게 임하면 불가능한 일은 없을거라고 믿는다. 게다가 난 아직도 내가 영어로 말하고, 읽고, 쓴다는 걸 믿을수가 없다. SAT를 준비하는 내 자신도 아직도 낯설기만 할 정도로 영어에 자신이 없었던 나, 이렇게까지 해온 내가 자랑스럽기만 하다. 엄마는 늘 말씀하신다. 네가 여기 미국에서 주저 앉으라고 하나님이 너를 미국에 보내지 않으셨다고. 지금은 부족해도 10년 후, 20년 후의 너를 보라고 말씀하신다. 궁금하다. 10년, 20년 후의 나는 다른 사람에게 어떤 영향을 주며 이 사회에 어떤 역할을 담당하고 있을지....

CONNECTED

Peter Choi (Won-Hyuk Choi)

It is impossible for all the human beings to remember what they did when they were one to two years old. But you can hear about your childhood from your parents and grandparents. And I am not an exception. I have no memories about my childhood, but I heard a lot about myself through my parents and my grandparents.

According to my mom (Jeanie Kim) and my dad (Harry Choi), I was born in Korea in the hospital, called Jae-Il Hospital on April 22, 1991. When I was born, before the nurses handed me over to my mother, I had my arms and legs stretched out, and I was waving them frantically, while other babies were calm and slept inside a blanket. In anticipation, every family member came and congratulated my birth.

Hundred days after my birth, I had a party to celebrate my 100th day. This is a special Korean tradition. During this "100th day birthday party", my parents put some objects, such as pencil, money, and book on the floor, as is Korean tradition. And then the baby is placed on the floor to grab one of these items. If the baby grabs the pencil, that means that when he grows up, he will become a professor. Money represents wealth, and the book represents intelligence. In this ceremony, I grabbed the pencil. I guess I was destined to become a professor of electrical engineering.

Few months after I was born, I moved to USA and lived there for about 4 years. We stayed in an apartment, called Rotonda in Virginia, and my father studied at the American University in Washington, D.C. for his

Bachelor's degree. My father majored in business economics.

When he went back to Korea after his Bachelor's degree, he started working at Sang-Up Bank. Eventually, the bank merged with other banks and became one of the most influential banks, called Woori Bank. Woori Bank expanded greatly and now has extended itself to USA with its headquarter in Manhattan, New York. Recently, a subsidiary of Woori Bank purchased the AIG building in New York for over 150 million dollars. My father is an executive in the New York headquarters, involved in the Woori Bank expansion in America. Woori Bank is the biggest Korean Bank in America, and many Koreans in USA are customers. The Korean community in New York and New Jersey are mostly Korean-speaking. Woori Bank is thriving in America because a large percentage of Koreans in America is small business owners, such as dry cleaners owners and vegetable store owners. When I finish my bachelor's degree in engineering, and go on and receive my PhD in engineering, I would like to be a professor, who owns a company that engineers electronic objects.

Now, I have great dreams for my future, and the reality to support my dream. When I was a baby, I was somewhat aware of my future destiny. I was a really quiet baby who did not cry often as other babies did. When my dad was driving with me in the car, he sometimes totally forgot about me and left me in the car. That's how quiet I was. My parents also said that I was a pensive boy. When I was 3 years old, I had to touch everything that I saw and tasted it. It was not really a good habit, but my parents say that I was an "extra care-required" boy. Another interesting fact about my childhood is that I made up a lot of the words and used it even when someone else corrected me. I called coke 'gieh', aunt 'moodoo', car 'ahkunka', helicopter 'ahkunta', squirrel 'pumbi' etc. It took awhile for my family members to figure out what I was talking about. When there was a car passing by, I would say "ahkunka, ahkunka…" My grandmother saw that and figured out that I was talking about car, and she tried to correct me by saying, "say car". I did follow what she said, but few minutes later I would start my own language again.

My childhood up to 4 years old was spent in Virginia, where my father was pursuing his Bachelor's degree, married to my mom. When I first went into a day care program in Virginia, I was a shy boy who did not know how to speak English at all. At first day of day care, I was so afraid that when I realized that my dad was leaving without taking me, I started to cry out and chase after him. My dad had to persuade me to stay with the kindergarten teachers. But even after I stopped crying, I was still afraid that I beat any kids who came close to me. It took a lot of effort for my parents to go around and say sorry to all the victims' parents. Although they did not want me to hurt anyone, they did not want to destroy my fighting spirit because they wanted me to be a corporate leader; so, they tried to maintain the balance in educating me.

My parents always remind me that I am one of the luckiest children in the world because I lived in so many different regions and traveled a lot. Also, they cared about me so much that they always gave me the best education possible, and taught all different kinds of useful skills. I started swimming when I was 5 years old, and I started to ski when I was 4 years old. Also, they took me to Hawaii, Guam, Canada, London, Washington, and New York, although I don't remember any of them. I lived in Seoul, Washington D.C, and Colorado.

When I went back to Korea with my father who finished his study at American University and moved to an apartment in Seoul, I was a lonely boy. I was too young to go to kindergarten or school, and I had no friends, so I was always alone. But, few days after we moved, my mom introduced me to the next door neighbor. Luckily, they had a child who was the same age as I. His name is Han Ju Yung. He had many interesting toys, so I went over to his house every day. He forced me to call him "hyoung", meaning older brother, just because he was 2 month older than I, but I refused.

This time of the year was the best for me because I had absolutely no grief at all and always played with my friends. I played tops, jump ropes, bicycles, and videogames. Also, my friends and I liked to hunt all kinds of bugs, such as dragon flies, in my neighbor hood. During winter, we made snowmen everywhere in the apartment, and had snowball fights.

The elementary school that I attended was called Gae-Sung Elementary School, which is a top private elementary school with 12% acceptance rate. My mom was so happy when I was the very first one who was accepted into the school. At that time, I didn't know what school was, so I congratulated my mom.

First day of school, I got into a fight with another 1st grader, Kim Hyun Soo, who just entered the school like me. The origin of the fight was really childish. The fight was to determine whether the ball I kicked went into the goal or not. We both cried but no one was injured. The fight was stopped when an upperclassman came up with a solution, which was to give me a penalty kick. However, as soon as I made the goal in, he started the fight again. As a result, my parents were called to the school. This was my first day of the school.

Now that I'm in high school, I don't understand why I hated my school that much. My worst class was the "morality class". I did not understand what they were talking about, and I always got yelled at by the teachers. However, even my homeroom teacher admitted the fact that I was good at math. Ever since then, math became my favorite subject.

When I advanced to 2nd grade, my dad gifted me with a puppy at kid's day, which is May 5th, every year in Korea. She was a small baby who was just born. We named her "Shu-shu" and gave her a lot of attention. After school, I spent my times training my dog and playing with her. She was little bit rough because she was a hunting dog, but she was not dangerous. My younger brother (Jonathan Choi) was mad at the fact that I was the one who trained Shu-shu, and he importuned my parents to buy him another dog. So another puppy named "Pini" came to our house, but she also did not give a lot of attention to my brother.

Besides my love of dogs, I had another love, namely soccer. Soccer has been my favorite ever since when I was 6 years old. I always played soccer with random kids in town, and I always was the best. I thought that I was so special that I once tried to climb up the tree and kick the soccer ball. When I was half way up, my hand slipped, and I crashed down on my head. Although I did not have a concussion, I was in great pain. I opened my house door with blood all over my shirt. My mom was so surprised but calmly called the hospital, and I stitched my wound up. But this was only the beginning. After this incident, I stitched up about 5 more times. All these scars are from sports. So, you can see I was a very tough kid with a fighting spirit. It is this spirit that will make my future.

When I turned into an 8th grader, my dad was appointed as an executive of Woori Bank in America, which was aggressively expanding in America. It was second time for me to live in USA. I first moved to East Chester, New York, which had no Koreans at all. Most of the Koreans then were living in Flushing, New York. In East Chester, I went to a school called Anne Hutchinson. I had forgotten all the English that I had learned in Virginia because I was too young when I had learned it. And in Korea, there was no opportunity to maintain the little English I had acquired during my dad's studies at American University. So, I had hard time communicating with my teachers and my classmates. Even in ESL, I was struggling tremendously. However, I was much better at soccer compared to everyone else in USA because Americans do not take soccer as seriously as Koreans do. Because Americans like athletic people, I made a lot of friends while playing soccer.

When I learned good enough English, my parents and I moved to Harrington Park, New Jersey, where I am living right now. We moved because my mom was lonely by herself. My dad wanted my mom to have some Korean friends, so we moved to a region where there are a lot of Koreans: Bergan County in New Jersey. For instance, there are so many Koreans in Old Tappan that out of 300 seniors at Old Tappan High School, about 100 of them are Korean. However, my life here has been just a pain in the ass. There is nothing going on around this region. We had to drive out to do something special. The town itself is only a place to live. I had nothing to do other than go to school, play some sports, and play computer games. The town is covered with trees, and there aren't any fast food restaurants. In order to go to the mall, we had to drive about 30 minutes.

My parents realized this situation and how I felt, so every summer in America, my parents sent me to a summer camp during the summer vacation. It was a whole new world for me because it had everything I wanted to try, such as water ski, rock climbing, paintball, MTV, and archery. Also, it was the first time for me to sleep outside without my parents, so it felt special. I met a lot of friends there that I still keep in touch with. They all had different nationalities; some were from Europe, some were from South America, and some were from Asia. Some of them were not able to speak English fluently, so we weren't able to exchange communication, but still we were good friends.

When I turned into a high school student at Old Tappan High School, my mom forced me to go to hakwon, which is a special Korean school where you learn and prepare for tests and SATs. From hakwon, I have learned mostly math and science to prepare for SAT 2's. As a result, I have received a very high score in SAT 2; 800 in Math Level 2 and 770 in Chemistry. Ever since the start of the high school life, my life has been really boring.

The only special thing is that during each summer vacation, I visit Korea. In Korea, I meet all of my old friends and hang out until the daybreak. I eat everything I want and do everything I want to do in Korea. The hamburgers I eat in Korea have different flavors and tastes from the ones in USA. Korean hamburgers are sweet and sugary, while American hamburgers are big and salty. Also, when I am in Korea, I go to karaoke whenever I meet with my friends. Furthermore, when I meet with friends who play computer games, we go to a special place called PC room. PC room is a place where there are about 50 PCs in a room, and people pay a dollar or two per hour to play computer games, surf the web, or do their homework. We usually play computer games. We also go to the cinema and watch Korean movies. We do not have to spend a lot of time moving around because all the buildings are crowded together, and Korea has a well organized subway. Also, the price of taxi is cheap, so even teenagers like us have no problem moving from one area to another without car.

As I have been hanging around with my friends, I noticed that I am somehow different from my friends. Whenever I go to a mall or restaurant, they ask me if I live in a foreign country. Whenever I ask them how they figured it out, they always reply back saying, "I don't know, but you have an aura that is different from ordinary Koreans." Some of my friends say that it is the way I dress, and some say it is the way I speak. Although I feel different from my friends, I still enjoy spending time with them. Right now, I can't wait until my visit to Korea, the next summer.

Dear Peter,

In 1991, I was gazing at a swaddled bundle of a newborn.
It is almost 20 years ago, but your image is still vivid in my mind.

When I took you out for golf this summer, my heart was full of mixed emotion. I was sad when I realized that I was too far from you, being separated by the Atlantic Ocean, to watch your teenage years, to see the process of your growth, every step of the way. I was happy when I noticed that you already became a young man of great promise. You were full of positive energy like me in the yearbook photos.

Despite all the pressure you might have, you are perfectly you. Young, beautiful, rough a lot like life. I hope that you will become an important leader In the future, I want you to remember, you just have to keep swinging and believe it will all even out in the end.

When I was a young man like you, I could only enjoy playing golf on the good days around good friends of mine. As I got older, I got to love golf little bit more even on the bad days. I believe you should play with more of your opponents than friends. You will learn that there are no winners or loser, victories or defeats. Playing the game with respect is the ultimate reward.

Do not lose your respect toward others and do not let them lose their respect toward you. Live well, my dear.

Soo-Sung Lee
Your Grand-Uncle
President, Seoul National University, South Korea
Former Prime Minister, Republic of Korea (South Korea)

OVERCOMING HARDSHIP

Hyun Seonwoo

My life has been very unpredictable, like a card game. Once I had all I wanted, but soon I lost it all. I was in a situation like a desperate card player who has to bet all the money one has. When a player is faced with insufficient remaining money to continue the game, he bets the remainder of his money and declares himself "all in". He may now hold onto his cards for the remainder of the deal. Like one card player who gives his all in a game to win desperately, I have bet my entire life. Coming to America was very risky, and it was like betting my life. I had nothing to bet on but my life, so I bet my life to win. I saw many obstacles that I would confront, and I knew I would have very small chance to succeed. However, I bet my entire life to win a game called "life."

My life started on March 6, 1991, in In-Cheon. I was not from a very wealthy or famous family, but from an ordinary family. I was the first son of father, Heon Seonwoo, and mother, Young Hee Oh. My father is a business man, and my mother is a housewife. Even though my parents are not geniuses or very special people, they are highly educated in colleges and graduate schools. My father graduated from Gun Guk University and my mother graduated Sung Shin Women's University. Therefore, their intelligence surrounded me since I was born. They knew that teaching alphabets or other subjects was not as important as giving me the opportunity to learn through a variety of experiences and showing me how to behave properly. As a result, I could learn through many experiences, which helped me to make me who I am.

Throughout my life, my father has influenced me greatly. I learn to overcome hardships, try my best, and do not give up on anything. My father was the last son of his family, different from my situation. However, since he was young, he had to go through many hardships. My father's family did not have sufficient money to have an extravagant lifestyle, but a frugal lifestyle. When he was in high school, he faced the most tragic event in his life. It was critical time for him because it was the time he should have focused on his academic works. However, he could not do it because of the illness of my grandmother. She suffered from diabetes. He had two older brothers, but my father was the only one who took care of her. My grandfather was not able to take care of her because he was also suffering from illness.

My grandfather was a congressman in the most chaotic time of politics of Korea. It was when Jung Hee Park, the president of Korea was a dictator over the entire country. However, my grandfather did not want dictatorship, but freedom in Korea. Yet, his dream was not fulfilled during his time. Also, he went through electrical torture because the president could do whatever he wanted to people, who went against him. As a result, when my father was in high school, my grandfather was in the hospital suffering from aftereffect of the electrical torture.

In the family, there was no one to provide for my father, so he had to tutor students to make money for his high school education. Also, he had to take care of grandmother. For about two years, my grandmother suffered and passed away, leaving behind my father. Even though my father had a blighted circumstance in which to study, he was a top student in his high school. As his classmate dreamed, he also wanted to go to Seoul National University: the best college in Korea. However, he could not enter Seoul National University, due to his financial circumstances. However, there was one college, which offered a full scholarship to my father: Gun Guk University.

Even though he received a full scholarship from the college, he had to work to provide the fee for the hospital where my grandfather was. Two older brothers of my father also contributed some money. He graduated from four years of college and went to a graduate school for business. After he graduated from the graduate school, my father met my mother and married. Also, he was employed by one of the four biggest companies (called "Chaebol") in Korea; namely, SK. He started to work as a new employee and became the deputy section chief of the company. I remember when my father went to work early in the morning in a suit. I was almost in a sleep, but woke up and saw my father off to work.

As an employee of a company, although the company was gigantic, my father was paid small amount of money. Most people would be satisfied with continuous payment from a company, but my father was not satisfied. As a man in age 38, most people do not want to face challenges, but my father quit his job as a deputy section chief in SK Company to start his own business. His business was to join a foreign company with a Korean company for a project, and he received profit from the project. His company's name was "Cyno21." One thing changed from when he worked for SK Company; he did not have to go to work early in the morning, and he did not have to dress up, every morning, because he was the owner of the company.

In several years, he established a very solid company. He earned more than enough money to support my family. As a result, when I was in elementary school, I had all I wanted. Whenever I went to a mall, if I wanted something, my father was able to buy it for me. We had a luxury car and a big house. Also, we went out to eat every weekend to a very expensive restaurant. When I was in a lavish circumstance, I did not realize how blessed I was. I thought that my life style was normal. Furthermore, I did not realize how hard my father had to work to provide all things that I had.

However, the lavish life of my family did not last too long. When I was in middle school, my father's company was bankrupted. As a result, my family did not have any money left. One of the workers of my father's company stole all the money needed for the company, so father did not have any money to maintain the business. My father had to claim bankruptcy. For several months, I did not see my father. I knew that my father was in despair and felt terrible about his failure. He went through such hard situations to be a successful owner of a company. However, he had to confront another cruel circumstance of his life. I do not know what my father did for several months after his bankruptcy, but I am sure that he remembered his past and revived the memory of the time when he was successful and the reasons for which he wanted to be successful. When my family finally met my father, even though my father's face was pale and his body was withered, we could see his smile again. He regained his strength and did his best to be successful again. Through my father, I think that I learned this the most: his courage and strength to overcome all the tragic hindrances he confronted throughout his life.

In a sense, I guess I have my father's fighting spirit. When I was born, I was in a fatal situation. An ordinary baby would be born in about 10 months, but I was born under 8 months. Therefore, my weight and my body function were lower than those of ordinary babies, so I was in a lethal situation. As a result, before I could be in my mother's arms, I was in a bed of Incheon Gil Hospital. Fortunately, I was able to recover myself, and my body function became normal after about 2 months of medical treatment. I think that this was why my parents took care of me with special care when I was young. If I caught a cold, all my family members were worried and took special attention on my recovery. Since I was weak when I was young, most time my mother prepared foods that I wanted to eat. Because of the efforts and cares of my families, when I was in Kyung In Kyo Dae Elementary school, I was one of the tallest kids, although now I am not the tallest kid in my class anymore.

Throughout my life, since my mother loved to travel, I could learn many things through traveling. Every summer and winter, my family traveled all over the Korea. As a result, there are only few places that my family have not visited in Korea. My family's traveling made winter my favorite season, because I could go skiing with my family. Since I was five, I learned and enjoyed skiing. My favorite ski resort was Yong Pyung. In order to enjoy skiing, I had to be patient for five hours, because it took me about five hours to get to the resort. As a child, I always complained whenever I was in the car on the way to the ski resort. Every time I went, I got better and better at skiing. I can't quite explain the feeling that I got from sliding down the mountain, as I faced the cold winter breeze.

However, there was one year that I could not go skiing. When I was eight, my family lost a precious person in the family, my other grandmother, Yeon Ok Yu. Still, my family does not know if my grandmother is alive or not, because we never saw her body. She was abducted when I was eight. Since she had been kidnapped, the sorrow of my family has been augmented. It was a cold winter day. My grandfather or my uncle used to pick her up from the fish market. Yet, on one December day, my grandfather and uncle could not go to pick her up, so she took a taxi. She was heading to a hospital where my aunt gave a birth to my cousin. That was all my family and I know about the abduction. Since I was young, I could not feel the pain as same as my mother did. My mother had lost her mom. I think that as a child, I was more disappointed because I could not go skiing. However, as I recall the moment now, my eyes become all wet. My grandmother always sacrificed herself for my family, and she never had time to rest or enjoys her life. I had never seen her wearing fancy clothes or buying something for herself. Several clothes with smell of fish were all she had, because she worked at a big fish market. She went to work at 6 am and came back at 9 pm and sold as many fishes as possible. That was her schedule from Monday to Saturday.

Working at a fish market was not an easy job for my grandmother. During the summer, because of the heat, the market filled with the smell of fish, and during the winter, the temperature decreased, so she had to fight the coldness. She lived her life like this for about 20 years. Working at a fish market was all she did. However, all I saw from my grandmother was smiles. She never complained about her life but ended her life tragically. If she had many times to take a rest and enjoy her life, I would not be so sorry for her. When I realized this, it was the first time I felt that the world is not fair for everyone, although most people say life is fair for everyone. This incident was the most tragic event in my life, and it helped me to mature. As I went through hard time, I thought that the tragic and sad moment of life mature and grow myself.

The loss of my grandmother influenced me enormously throughout my childhood. I could not get rid of all the sorrow I had. I remember, most days, I cried before I went to sleep. Also, I was able to be mature because of the abduction, and I tried my hardest at everything because I wanted to be a successful man and find criminals who abducted my grandmother. In addition, I knew that my grandmother was watching me from the heaven, so I did not want to disappoint my grandmother. My determination became the foundation of my personality. Although I tried to be strong, sometimes I could not hide the sorrow. When

I was in fourth grade, my friend brought a toy, and I asked him where he got it. He said that he got it from his grandmother as his birthday gift. As I heard the word "grandmother," I just started to cry. I think I never cried like that in front of my teacher and classmates before or ever since. I did not know why I was crying. I thought I forget all the sorrows I used to have. Yet, my heart still remembered the sorrow that I had. I could not hide my sadness, which filled my entire heart.

My crying in front of everybody shocked some people. I was usually a happy and active person. I went to Kyung In Kyo Dae Elementary school located in Soong Eui Dong, Incheon. I remember, at the first day of the school, on March 1998, I was a diffident boy who was too shy to hold hands with a girl partner who stood right next to me. Yet, through some times and experiences, I became a mature student, who could associate with every person in the class, and a student who could lead one class. In Korea, from the third grade onward, they pick a president and a vice president for each class. Class president is a representative and the leader of one class. Other than class president and vice president, there is a president and a vice president for the entire school. One should be a fifth grader or a sixth grader, in order to be a vice president for the entire school. Also, only a sixth grader could be a president for the entire school.

In the third grade, I was one of the candidates for the class president. But I could not be a president because of my innocence. The difference of vote for the winner and me was just one vote, which was mine. I thought I had to write the name of a candidate other than my name, so I did not vote for myself. Therefore, I became a vice president for the class. This precious experience taught me that I have to always vote for myself, and I never made the same mistake again. As a result, I was the president of my 4th grade class.

In fifth grade, I was able to become a vice president of the entire school. Yet, it was not an easy job to keep, and it was very different from being a president for a class. I had to be very careful in the school with my behavior, attitude, and speech. Sometimes, I had to give the morning announcement. It was a very hard task to do, and every time I did it, I was very nervous. However, this experience matured me to be a leader, and a better person than I was before. Also, it opened a way of becoming the president for my school, a year later.

Before the voting day, my opponent, Hyun Ju Kim, and I did our best to become the president, and the process was very intense. Yet, Hyun Ju and I really tried hard not to insult each other like real candidates criticizing each other, because we were friends. On the voting day, I was really nervous, although I told others that I really do not care about the result, deep down in my heart, there was a small passion and desire of wanting to be the president. Later, I found out that I became the president of the whole school. There was a huge gap between my vote and Hyun Ju's. I could not show my happiness because I knew that she would feel worse, if she saw me smiling and enjoying being a winner. Since I was the president, I took part in lots of events and had many privileges that I would not have had if I had been just an ordinary student. However, as I had more privileges as a leader, there were more responsibilities.

I remember one of my friends, Bum Jin Jung, who was a year younger than I was. Before I became a president I said to students that I would make a store in school. Different from USA, where one can buy drinks and cookies from a snack stand, in Korean schools, one cannot buy anything. This issue was not a small one which I could solve, but I said to students that I would make it happen. Then, after I became a president, Bum Jin, whenever we meet, asked me when I was going to make the school store. I was so sorry and embarrassed that I could not keep the word I had given. As a result, I always avoided him throughout the rest of my elementary school.

In school, I was never a genius but an intelligent student who did his best at every work. That was what my parents taught me. They wanted me to be a person who always tries one's best, not a lethargic genius. As a result, I was one of teachers' favorite students. As years went by, and I received my grades, I realized that my parents were right, and it felt really good when I received good grades. Since then, I think I worked hard every time to achieve what I used to have. However, I always did not get what I expected or deserved, because of my clumsiness. Moreover, some of my friends started to get tutors, but my mother never thought of getting me a tutor. As a result, I had to try twice as hard as my friends to achieve better grades. Later, trying hard became my habit and always I tried my hardest in everything that I did; whether musically or academically.

On the graduation day of my elementary school, February 2003, I was very depressed because I had to leave the school I had attended for six years and the people I had loved. As I gave a speech to my classmates and teachers as the school student body president, I recalled all the memories I had from my elementary school. Even a bad memory was pleasant to me as I left my beloved school. On the other hand, I was excited. I knew that it was the start of a long journey. I knew that there would be more interesting events that I would confront.

I had many memories during my elementary school. I think, sometimes, that all the happy memories I had were during my elementary school. One of my happiest memories was traveling. Since my mother loved to travel, I went on a trip a lot. The first airplane I took was to Japan in 2001. Since it was the first time, I was very nervous, but I got used to circumstances in an airplane, I enjoyed being in an airplane. Also, I loved an airplane, because I could have free soda, whenever I wanted to drink. Japan was a very quiet country compared to Korea. I was surprised because drivers never honked the horns, but in Korea, wherever I was, I always heard the sound of horns. The city I went to was not a rural area, but the capital of Japan, Tokyo, so I was surprised. That was my first impression of Japan. Since I arrived with people in a tour group, I had to follow their schedules. Since I was young, and the organization's purpose for this trip was education, I mostly went to museums and Japanese temples. I remember Japanese Technology Museum and Natural History Museum. Also, I remember uncountable numbers of temples in Japan. I did not learn much from the temples, but I thought they were well constructed, architecturally.

Different from what I expected, the Japanese environment and Japanese hotels were very clean, and the scenery was awesome. The most exciting event was visiting Disney World in Japan. Japan has been called "the country of imitation." They imitated many things from other countries, and Japanese Disney World was one of them. I've never been to real Disney World; however, the one in Japan fascinated me. They had everything that I loved: games and roller coasters. My favorite ride was a falling boat. Not only the feeling I got when the boat dropped from up high to down low excited me, but also the splashing of water when the boat reached the bottom was awesome. I was surprised by how Japanese could emulate the Disney World.

I used to abhor the Japanese because of the conflict between Korea and Japan in history, and the conflict continues to the present day. I learned about the cruelty and the malice of the Japanese through learning what they had done to my ancestors when they took over Korea (1910-1945). They killed thousands of ancestors. The most horrible story I heard was that one Japanese soldier cut off a Korean woman's breast. By the soldier's action, the woman died and a baby died also, because the baby could not be fed through the breast of the mother. Moreover, Japan even changed the spelling of Korea. It was supposed to be Corea, but since "C" was in front of "J" of Japan, Japanese changed the English spelling to Korea, so that Japan could go before Korea during Olympic games. In the present day, Korea and Japan's conflict has continued. Korea and Japan are fighting for the ownership of an island located in an ocean between Japan and Korea, Dok Do, because the owner of the island is the owner of the ocean. Who "owns" the part of the ocean where the island is being fiercely contested. As a result, I really did not like the Japanese. However, this trip alleviated my hatred toward these people because I saw the difference from what I had learned.

A year later, I had another chance to visit Japan again; I visited a different location from where I've been to before. Hukuoka was similar to Tokyo, but Tokyo was more developed city than Hukooka. Also, I went there with different people. I went to Japan with my friends, Su Yeol Lee, Min Pyo Hong, Bo Ram Kim, Bo Yun Choi, Hyun Ju Kim, Bum Jin Jung and our parents. We have friends since the beginning of elementary school. We went on trips together many times, but it was our first time to travel a foreign country together. It was a great trip, because I was able to travel to a different country with my close friends and share experiences with them. I cannot forget this trip because I made so many precious memories with my friends through this trip. Even though some places was not so attractive to us, since we were together, every place we visited was great and pleasant. Above all, I think the hotel was my favorite place in this trip, because I could talk and have fun with my friends. We stood up all night and just talked and played, so although I enjoyed my other part of the trip, being in the hotel with my friends was my favorite time of the journey. But there were some cool, fun places to visit during the Japan trip, such as Universal Studio in Hukuoka, Japan. The real one's in USA but they also imitated this one, too. Yet, it was great, and I had a lot of fun with my friends. There were rollercoaster rides centering on famous movies, such as E.T. and Jurassic Park. Through this trip, I was able to strengthen my friendship with my friends and learned about new cultures, which I did not know before.

A year later, I had one more opportunity to go to Japan. It was just a family trip. Even though I already had visited Japan twice, every time I visited, it was different. In addition, since the third time was a family trip, it was a special experience. We went to a huge resort called "House Tenbo," which was like a big castle. In the resort, I could use bike to travel. Also, there was a bike for 4 people to ride together, and this was very interesting. Since it seemed very different from what I usually used, my family and I took the bike for 4 people. It was new experience for me, and through this trip, my skill in bike riding was augmented. Also, there was a bike with a turbo button. I really like how the Japanese made new products to satisfy a variety of customers. In the resort, I watched a laser show and took a boat to see the night scenery of the beautiful resort. Since, I was with my family, I was in comfort.

These three trips to Japan changed my prejudice toward Japanese. I realized that I should not judge the Japanese by history, but by who they are now. Also, I started to feel that Korea wasn't the only place on earth, and the world is larger than where I lived. Therefore, I decided to set my goal, which could influence the whole world, not just Korea.

Although my trip to Japan was interesting and fabulous, my trip to Europe was the most exciting trip. When I was in fifth grade, in 2002, my family and I went to France, Switzerland, Italy, Germany, Belgium, and England for fifteen days. These six countries had their own characteristic and attraction, which fascinated my mind. Since there was no guide and we could go anywhere we wanted, this trip was special. However, there were many problems at first. First of all, we couldn't speak their languages, even English. The only way we could communicate was using our hands and bodies to express our thoughts. We depended on a map and started the travel in the order of France, Switzerland, Italia, Germany, Belgium, and England. We didn't eat great food there, because only restaurant we knew was McDonald's. However, I had unforgettable memories from this trip.

Before I went to Paris, I had a high expectation to the city, called "the city of art." Whenever I thought of Paris, I always imagined a clean and sophisticated city. However, when I went to Paris, the city was the opposite of my expectation. I took a train in the city, but it was very messy and malodorous. I was so disappointed. Yet, I, soon, realized why the city was so renowned and beloved by people. I went to the most famous museum, Louvre Museum. It had so many famous and beautiful paintings, which fascinated my eyes. I was surprised about the fact that I could enjoy many famous paintings in one place. Especially, I loved the genuine Mona Lisa. Also, I went to the Palace of Versailles. The palace was so beautiful that I couldn't keep my eyes away from the palace. Later, I was able to see Eiffel Tower. It was huge and beautiful. When I went up the tower, I realized why the tower is famous. Then, I visited Notre Dame Cathedral. It was a colossal cathedral. I wanted to go to the top of the cathedral. Since there was no elevator, I had to walk up the stairs. It was the hardest part of my trip, but when I reached the top and saw the cathedral and the city, my resentments disappeared. Also, I saw Arc de Triomphe. It was a symbol of victory for Napoleon. On the top, I was able to see the entire city. Through these beautiful places, I realized why people loved this city and called this city the city of art.

After my family spent two days in Paris, we took a train to Switzerland. Taking train to each country was one of my favorite parts of the journey. I had never taken a train with a bed. I was surprised because the train consisted of rooms with 6 beds. It was quite a new experience to me. Switzerland was the same as my expectation. The country was very clean, and cities were surrounded with trees, lakes and mountains, which provided very beautiful scenery. In Switzerland, I went to the Alps. Since the mountain was very elevated, we went to the top by taking a mountain train. Even though it was summer, there was snow and it was very cold, so I had to wear long sleeves shirts. Since it was a very elevated place, my head was dizzy, and it was hard to breathe. However, I could never forget the scenery I saw from the top of the mountain. It was fantastic. I also went to a famous chapel in Switzerland. It was a beautiful chapel, which was surrounded by the beautiful scenery of Switzerland. In Switzerland, I felt the greatness from the gift of environment.

After the journey in Switzerland, my family went to Italy. At first, my family was kind of scared. When we went there, it was right after the 2002 World Cup, and Korea defeated Italy in the quarterfinal. At that time, I heard rumors that Italian people hated Koreans. I was wearing a Korean soccer Jersey, which read, "Be the Reds," with red color, which symbolized the Korean soccer team. Also, I heard a story of how Italian people did not like Korean after World Cup; one Korean store in Italia was attacked by a frantic fan. Even though I was scared, I wore the Korean Soccer jersey, but no one hurt me, although there were some people, who gave me fierce looks. However, as times went by, I fell in love with Italy. In Italy, the traces of glorious history, and traces of the present coexisted. In the well-developed city of Rome, I could see a sanctuary, which was built about a thousand years ago. I went to the Coliseum. After thousands of years have passed, it has still preserved its great value. I could not go inside of it because there was a huge line in front of the Coliseum. We also visited Rome's renowned churches. Later, I went to Trevi Fountain. Like from a famous movie, my family and I went to the fountain with ice creams. It was a beautiful fountain. Also, Vatican City in Rome was very interesting. I was surprised by the concept of a city in a city.

In the Vatican City, there was a huge Catholic church. I went inside of it and was very moved by it. I hoped to see the Pope in the Vatican City, but as I expected, I could not meet him. I saw many famous artifacts, which I used to see in a history book. As I saw the artifacts and many historical sites, I was able to feel how great Rome was in history. Also, I went to Venice, a city surrounded by water. At Venice, there were no cars, but boats were the only transportation. Everything I did in Italy was new experiences.

The next country I visited was Germany. Germany was a very well-developed country. Since they had a reputation as a highly developed technology center and a science leader, I went to many science museums. One museum I remember is Air Craft Museum. They had all the air planes starting from World War I to the present day. As

I saw the air planes, I realized the highly developed technology of Germany. Also, I could see the traces of World War I and World War II in many museums. As I walked through their markets, I could see their cultures and customs that were different from mine. Since my mother heard that Germany had good kitchen knives, we walked around about 5 hours to buy a kitchen knife. When we bought it, I did not realize why this knife is better than others, because I do not use it. However, I could see my mother's happy face toward the knife. Later, we moved to the next destination, Belgium.

Because Belgium was on the way to England from Germany, we went to Belgium. However, we did not have much time, so we did not spend lots of time in Belgium, so I did not go to many places as I had in other countries. I went to a big market, and other places where I could see how Belgian people live. Even though I did not do many things in Belgium, I fell in love with this country. Also, I ate famous Belgian chocolates, and it really satisfied me. I thought the chocolate was the favorite part of the Belgium journey.

Last country I visited in this trip was England. When I went to Buckingham Palace, I felt solemn. The palace was enormous and was very ornate. Even though Queen of England did not have same power as in the past, the palace preserved the great power of the queen. Also, my family and I walked around the London city. The city was very crowded. When I saw the city from the London Eye, it was fabulous. I could see the London Bridge and all the famous architectures. Later, I went to the British Museum. It contained all the artifacts and famous remains of history from all around the world. I was surprised by how one museum could have the remains from different countries. My mother told me that the British Museum was the symbol of their greatness and glory from the history. Since they colonized so many countries, they were able to obtain such large amount of remains of history. I realized that British people cherish their great history and are proud of who they are. I only stayed for three days in London; I saw why people say that London is a great city.

The Europe tour taught me lots of things. Once again, I experienced how big the world is. Also, I learned to respect others' cultures that I haven't heard of, because they had their own way of living. Also, this trip crushed the wall between Europe and me. I had thought that they were really different from Koreans, but as I visited their countries, I realized that only some customs were different, and we're just same, human. Later, I came to realize that this Europe trip eventually led a way to USA.

In the winter of 2002, I had a chance to visit Canada. I went to Vancouver. Vancouver was really clean and quiet, but sometimes I felt depressed by the quietness. Also, the sun set earlier, so the darkness came earlier than other places. In addition, during the days I stayed in Vancouver, it was rainy most of the days. Therefore, my depression was augmented in Vancouver. However, I had really fun and new experiences. First week, my family visited the Rocky Mountains. In winter, the mountain was covered with snow. Snow was clear white. When I looked at the mountain, it felt like my heart was being cleansed. I've never seen a bigger mountain range than Rocky Mountain's. It would be nice too, if I visited there at summer.

After the first week at Rocky Mountain, my mother went back to Korea, and my sister and I stayed in Canada to learn English. It was my first time to learn English with native speakers of English. Also, it was my first time for a home stay. I didn't stay at a hotel, but I stayed at an ordinary house in Vancouver with a Canadian family. The family consisted of father, mother, and two sons. At first, it was really awkward, living with a different family, but I got used to it later, and became friendly with them. For about three weeks, I went to an English academy in Vancouver. Yet, the classes were filled with Koreans. I was nervous at first, but I made some friends and learned to speak English. Even though in three weeks, I didn't master English, it was my precious experience at a different country, speaking with different people in English. I think these three weeks alleviated my fear of speaking in English and speaking with non-Korean people. As a result, I still cannot forget what I did and learned for three weeks. Three weeks passed by very rapidly, and I was very depressed because I had to leave. I think that since then, I had a dream of studying abroad with different people and in different language from my Native Korean language.

My next trip was to USA. Before the summer of 2003, I visited many countries in the world, but I had not been to the world's most famous country, USA, so I had been a little disappointed. Yet, I finally had a chance to visit USA with my family in the summer of 2003. My first destination was JFK airport, New York, but the next day, I went to Boston. In Boston, I went to lots of famous places, such as Fenway Park, Freedom Trail, and Museum of Science. Yet, I remember one place clearly. It was Harvard University. I've heard of this university since I was young as the world's best school. I went there and saw people lying down on the grass and reading books. Every student I saw was reading or studying. The scene of students reading on the grass impressed me.

Our next destination was Niagara Fall. My family took a boat to get close to the fall. At the beginning, I didn't know why people were wearing raincoats, but I realized when I got closer to the fall. As I got closer to the fall, I got wet. It was an unforgettable scene. Huge amount of water was falling from the top of the fall. At night, I saw the fall with the lights, and it was the most beautiful thing I've ever seen. I realized why this fall became one of the world's most famous places. Next day, my family went to Canada. I went to the west coast of Canada a year ago, and we were at the east side of Canada, this time. Canada was very quite and clean. We went to the capital of Canada. The combination of sophisticated buildings and beautiful environment was very impressive. Also, I went to Quebec. In Quebec, I found traces of France, and many people spoke French. My experience in Canada was also pleasant as my experience in USA.

My life after the trip to USA was the worst of all time because that was the time my father confronted bankruptcy. My family and I were so depressed and were in despair. I had never thought I would be in this situation at that time, because I was always in affluent circumstances where I could get what I wanted, and I could do what I wanted. However, I had to change my pattern of my life to save anything I could save, and don't buy whatever I didn't need.

My father had a pretty solid company. He was a good leader of the company and had great vision. However, when we went to USA, one of the workers in my father's company took most of the money from the company and ran away with all the money. The amount of the money was pretty substantial, and this was needed to keep running the company. As a result, my father's company had to face bankruptcy. The effect of the bankruptcy was pretty immense. The things I watched on TV really happened in my life. Some people who lend money to my father came to my house and asked for the money. Of course, they weren't polite at all. They were so cruel and brutal when they came to my house. I wanted to yell at them, but as I saw my mother's face I couldn't do anything but listen to them. I was in middle school and was 14, so I could understand the situation. However, my little brother was 9. He shouldn't have been there and shouldn't have listened to them. At his age, he should see great things in the world, and watch cartoon or something. Yet, he was there, when the people came to my house and screamed for the money. When I was 9, I didn't face any situation like that. I was a premature kid, who liked to play soccer and play with toys. Therefore, I was so sorry for my brother. Also, I was mad because there was nothing I could do.

For about six months we couldn't see our father. Since, the people who lend the money wanted to see him and get money, he didn't come to the house, so they couldn't come into our house. During the six months, the entire family lost weight. I think that it was because we were so depressed and couldn't eat well. Also, since we didn't have lots of money, our menu didn't comprise of any meat. It was my worst period of time in my life. I couldn't even breathe well in my house. The depressed atmosphere suffocated me. Yet, I had to stay strong, because I was the oldest one of my siblings. I had to take care of my mother, sister and brother, instead of my father. This job wasn't easy. I, also, had to do well in my school, so the pressure was increased. Since then, I think my mother had very high expectations of me. She wants me to do well in school and go to a good college, and get a nice job. She regards it as a successful life. Therefore, I had to try harder than others and get much bigger pressure than others.

After six months, we saw my father again, and we all cried. My father became lean, and looked awful. Even though we lost lots of things we had, our family became closer to each other. Also, there were more conversations in the family. Because my father had more time to spend with us compare to before, there was more time that the family could spend together. In addition, each family member started to be more careful and thoughtful to each others. Despite losing all the money, we found peace and happiness in our family. That had been my hope during my worst time. Before that, I couldn't find any hope. The depressed atmosphere and despair surrounded me. I couldn't find anything that would make me happy. Yet, from the family, after my father's return, I could finally be happy and saw the hope. If I did not find any hope during that time, I might not have been able to write this story. At that time, I was so desperate, and just wanted to die. I thought dying was better than living, because each day was hell to me, and death seemed to me more comfortable. However, as I saw my family, my father, my mother, my sister, and my brother, I realized my thought was wrong. Even though I might have to go through hard time, if there are people who love me and have faith in me, I have to live and do my best in every time.

My determination for my life made me become a better student. Even though I was in plight-filled circumstance, I was able to do better than most students in my middle school. In my middle school, Yeon Sung Middle School, I was doing well. Even though all my friends were able to pay for tutors and academies for extra help, I couldn't find the finances to go to such places, but had to study by myself. It was very hard to understand and do all the works by myself, but I did my best at every work I did. In the middle school, there were 525 kids in my grade. I wasn't the top 1 rank in my school. Yet, I was number five in my grade. I was pretty satisfied, but deep in my heart, I wanted to achieve more than a fifth place. Some of my teachers recognized my efforts, and cheered me up. Also, my homeroom teacher suggested me to run for a vice president position for the school student body. Although I was the class president in 7th grade, I thought there's difference between class president and school student body vice president. According to my experience in the elementary school, if one becomes the vice president of the school, one should spend some money for the student body, so it's better to have a wealthy vice president. Therefore, I strongly refused to run for the vice president position. First of all, I didn't want to burden my parents, and I really thought it would be better to have a wealthier student to be a vice president for the good of the school and the students there. I told my teacher about my situation. Yet, still, she wanted me to be the vice president. My teacher insisted and said that there would be no economic burden to my family. I gave in to my teacher and ran to be a vice president. I prepared for the election with the least amount of money I could spend. Most works were done by hands of my friends, instead of paying someone to do it. I was really thankful to my classmates, when they did their best to support me. I could never forget their efforts. With the supports of my friends, teachers, and my family, I was elected the vice president for my school.

Although it seemed to others that I achieved many things, I was still up for the challenges and wanted to learn more. I also felt I still lacked lots of things. During this time, two of my friends went abroad to study. I envied them because they could get more chances to learn. I think that was when I started to think of coming to USA to study, although my situation was not sufficient to support it. I told my mother about my idea. To me, Korea was not a right place to learn about the world. Korea was too small to understand the world. Therefore, I really wanted to study in USA, the center of the world.

Even though my friends' moving to different country influenced my decision, it was not the only reason I had. I think that because I had nothing in Korea, it was easier to make my decision. Although I was the vice president, and a good student, I still was eager to achieve more than that. My goal wasn't to be a doctor in a small town of Korea, but to be a doctor who can work for the people in the whole world. My goal wasn't to go to a college in Seoul, Korea, but to go to a college that I could learn many things at a high level, like the Ivy League. Therefore, I wanted to start again fresh in USA. It was a very hard decision that my family made. Yet, my mother and father had faith in me and believed in me, so they agreed to my proposal. At that time, I did not really understand how much my parents sacrificed for me and my siblings.

It did not take me a long time to realize how much sacrifice my parents made for me and my siblings. Since, my father could not come because he thought he would make more money in Korea than he would in USA, my mother came alone with us. As a result, I realized that she's lonely and unsettled without my father. The absence of my father was not the only fact that made my mother's life worse. Since she could not speak English, there was no one to talk to. She didn't have any friends and couldn't shop by herself. All the circumstances suffocated her, and I could see the miserable time that my mother was having. Therefore, I had to do my best and try my hardest to achieve what I dreamed.

My family decided to stay in a small, two bedroom house in Ridgefield, New Jersey. I had a very hard time in the first two years in the United States because I couldn't understand or speak English. It was like torture not communicating with others. Whenever I went outside, I couldn't speak to anyone. Sometimes, I met my Korean friends and could have conversation with them. Yet, I wanted to speak with anyone I met freely, like I did in Korea. I think that the reason why I couldn't speak to people was that I had fear of speaking in English. I recovered my confidence and tore down my fear as I learned English, and met many people in the school. It took me about two years to speak English fluently, although still I'm not a perfect speaker.

However, it wasn't easy to get what I wanted. I couldn't do things like I imagined. The reality was harsh. Since I couldn't speak English, there was no way to do well in the class. In Korea, I was a top student, who was envied by my classmates, but I wasn't anymore in USA. It seemed all students in my class were better than I was. Yet, I couldn't just give up. It was just a start, and there were lots of people who had faith in me, so I tried my hardest in every work. As a result, I passed my ESL class in 5 months.

However, passing ESL class wasn't the end of my dream. There were numerous steps I had to climb.

High School was a new start, but on the other hand, it was a new obstacle I had to overcome. In freshmen year, I was still confused and didn't know what I had to do. Still, my English wasn't good enough. As a result, I couldn't take many honors classes; only the math honor class. Because I was pretty good at math, I took the math honors class, since middle school. At that time, I thought that I didn't really care about honor classes, but as times went by, I realized that honors classes provide a higher level of studying and tackle more challenging materials. So, I really wanted to take more honors classes. To achieve my goal, I tried harder. In my sophomore year, I entered into the chemistry honors class. However, I couldn't get into other two honors classes. It was because of my English. Since my essay writing wasn't great and I still had a lot to learn about English, I couldn't get into the English honors class and the history honors class. It really hurt me, because I thought if I were in Korea, I would get into all honors classes that I wanted to take. Since I came to USA, there were only incidents that lowered my self-esteem.

I found relief and peace through Christ. I wasn't a Christian until I came to USA. I used to go to a Buddhist temple in Korea because my grandfather went to temples. However, many people I knew told me that in USA, I should go to the church. The main reason why I went to a Korean church was to meet new people and get help from the community. I started to go to New Garden Presbyterian Church. As times went, I found peace in the Christ and came to have faith in him. The Christian faith held me firmly, and I was able to endure all the pressures and obstacles.

During my high school years, I went to two missions trips. I didn't know much about the nature of mission trips, but as I went on the trips, I experienced the love of God and became closer to him. My first mission trip was to Washington, D.C., in the summer of 2007. I went there to spread the word of God to homeless people. I talked to them, gave them lunch, told them about the gospel of Christ. Ironically, Washington, D.C., which was supposed to be the center of the world's strongest countries, had countless homeless people. I thought that the capital of USA would be different or more developed than other cities. Yet, the parks I went to were filled with homeless people who were waiting for their lunch. There were many people with different stories of their lives. However, they had one similarity. They were in despair. Yet, they were recovering slowly under the cares of others. They found their confidence and hope again through Christ.

At Washington D.C, I met one guy who lived as a homeless person for a couple of years. He used to do drugs, so his pinky was paralyzed. Yet, he had a dream of being a pianist. Therefore, he started to practice piano and became a pianist. He was poor, but he recovered his dream, and found happiness. Even though he couldn't use his pinky, because it was paralyzed (so the song might not be the best in technical ways), the music he played was the most beautiful that I've ever heard. I didn't hear the melody through my ear, but through my heart. The melody was absorbed into my heart. However, soon I heard that he had only 6 months to continue his dream. He was fighting with cancer, and had about 6 months left. Had he pursued his dream when he was young, he would have been able to fulfill his life, but when he realized what he really wanted, he was too weak. However, he did not lose smile on his face. As I heard the song and looked at him, I realized that I was in a better situation than he was in, so I shouldn't give up my goal, but try to reach my goal. Also, I realized how powerful the love of God is and experienced his great love, myself.

My second mission trip was to Honduras in the summer of 2009. I went to Honduras with Dong San Alliance Church. I had never heard of this country before I went there. Before I went, I was afraid of going to a different country because I knew I would not be able to communicate with other people, which had different cultures. Also, Honduras was politically unsettled, and had a coup d'état. Yet, when I returned from Honduras, I didn't regret my decision of going to Honduras, but felt blessed about having gone to Honduras.

On the first day of my arrival in Honduras, I was surprised by the humidity and the heat. Even though it was morning, it was still hot. The heat lessened my determination to do my jobs.

I had two jobs to complete in Honduras: one was to teach kids in Honduras English, art crafts and the Bible, and my second job was to draw a wall painting at the school for the kids in Honduras. I was so nervous because I couldn't speak Spanish fluently. Also, I was thinking about kids in New Jersey or New York, who are very immature and different from the kids in Honduras. Yet, my fear disappeared when I met the kids. I could see their faces with happiness and innocence. As I looked at them, I found my courage to speak and teach them. Even though I couldn't speak to them perfectly, we were communicating with our hearts. I knew what they wanted, just looking at their faces. Of course, I couldn't make them perfect at English, but I was able to give them great experiences of learning English. The times I spent with them were unforgettable. As I got closer to them, I was surprised by their innocence. When I gave them candies and sandwiches, they were so thankful to me. Also, they were so happy when I made them paper airplanes. If I were a kid, I wouldn't be satisfied with candies or paper airplanes. However, they were so happy about such small presents.

Each minute I spent with them was precious and made me happy. During this time, I thought that although they are not wealthy and eat every day, they might be happier than I am, or people in USA. In USA, each day is a competition, and such lives within competition often suffocate people. People struggle through the day to be in a higher rank or earn more money, but they don't really find the real happiness that kids in Honduras have. They were free from all the agonies. I envied how they lived, and wished that I had been born like them, as a carefree child.

In the morning and afternoon, I spent time with kids at schools. After school, my team and I went to the walls at the school to draw pictures. We thought sketch would be the hardest part of the painting. Yet, someone had a brilliant idea. We used projector to show pictures at the walls and followed the lines. Therefore, we could draw quicker and more accurately. I thought painting would be an easy job to do. However, the hot weather of Honduras was a huge obstacle. While we were painting, we got sun burn all around our body. Sun block didn't work well under the blazing sun for several hours. Our team didn't have anyone who had a specialty or skill in drawing, but we finished the walls with beautiful painting because we knew that many kids will see the painting for many years. Then, they would build their dreams in the school, and may be later they will do the same job of service as I had done for them. I realized that what I had done wasn't the end but a start. The drawings, knowledge, and dreams that I gave to these kids will grow, and they will spread the hopes and dreams they saw to the world.

My trip was heading to the end. Before I came to USA, we had last time with kids we taught. They seem to know that it was the last meeting. They were also in a sad mood. We played soccer together and other games that made our time more precious and happy. After that, the kids said "Gracias" to our team. Every member started to cry when they heard that word. The kids' innocence and kind heart touched our team. It was a great moment. My eyes were also filled with tear.

My trip to Honduras was very special. I felt very settled throughout the journey. Every person that I met during the trip became special. I didn't know that I could be a person who eould be very emotional and a person to show my affection to others. I found my different self during my trip to Honduras. I went there to help people in Honduras, but I think they helped me to be happier and feel blessed. The love they showed to me was bigger than the love I gave to them. I really will not forget the precious time I spent during my summer in Honduras. In a sense, my love for mission trips and helping others replaced my love for sports.

Starting from the freshmen year, I started to join sports teams. In the fall, I joined the soccer team. In the winter, I joined the track team, and in the spring, I joined the tennis team. I joined sports teams, because I loved sports. Also, I wanted to lose my weight and get in shape. Furthermore, I wanted to make new friends through sports. I thought it was the better way to get close to others.

I wasn't always the best at everything. I was in a soccer team throughout my high school years. Yet, I wasn't a part of my high school varsity team since my freshmen year I played JV. Some of my friends were athletic and got four year varsity letter, but I couldn't, because I wasn't the best. However, I tried hard to reach the top. In my sophomore year, I was still in the junior varsity team, but in my junior year, I finally made my high school varsity soccer team. Still, I wasn't a starting member of the team. But in my senior year, I was one of the starting members of my soccer team. In track, I could see the improvement. As I practiced, the time for 100m and 200m decreased.

Tennis was the same. I started tennis the summer before my freshmen year. Therefore, I wasn't a good player, but I still was good enough to make the team, although the try-out was pretty competitive. However, I was an alternate member of the team, but I improved as times went by. In my sophomore year, I was 3rd single of my high school junior varsity team. Then, in my junior year, I was 1st double of my high school varsity team. It was a huge improvement. Coach Fabiano and my friends were surprised by my improvement. I was surprised, myself. Since I worked hard to achieve what I wanted, I could be closer and closer to the goal.

Not only in sports was I improving, but also in academics as well. In 8th grade, I passed the ESL, but I couldn't pass the English part of New Jersey state test, because I had taken it 3 months after I arrived in America. As a result, in freshmen year, I had to take English skills class. Yet, I passed this class with A+. Also, I received A in my English class in 9th grade. In the sophomore year, I had a regular schedule like the others because I passed my English skills class. I could see that my English was getting better. In my junior year, I took the English honors class. I thought that it was a harder class than regular classes, so I stepped up for the challenges, and I earned A- in that class. However, to earn the grade, I had to go through lots of troubles. It took me longer times to read a book and to write an essay than others, so I had to stay up until late into the night to do my homework. Also, some of my teachers and my friends laughed at me, when I said I'm in honors English. I was pretty embarrassed and mad at the same time that I should hear their taunts. However, by the end of the year, I proved that they were wrong to think that I was not good enough for honors English. Even though I still have some grammar issues and other problems in English, definitely, my English is better. It was such a hard job to improve the language skills, but I did. If I was the best at the beginning, I wouldn't try my hardest. Since I was at the bottom, I tried my hardest to climb the wall.

I know this will not be changed. Anywhere I go or whatever I do, I want to be a person who tries one's hardest to reach the top. My final goal of my life is to be a doctor, to help others. I have a very specific goal. I wanted to build a hospital that does not charge any patients in a third world country. As I read a biography of Albert Schweitzer, I realized that a doctor should not exist to make money or satisfy his own desires. However, a doctor should exist to help others and sacrifice himself to save others. It was what Schweitzer demonstrated throughout his life in Africa. In order to reach my dream, I have to try my hardest to become a good doctor, because I want to give the best care and treatment to future patients. There will be lots of works and obstacles that I have to overcome, but I will not give up on anything, because I already learned that giving up will not make my dream come true through my past 18years of life. Different from others', my life was very unpredictable. Even though I suffered a lot, I learned many lesson and matured through hardships. I know that hardships that I had been through will give me strength. Now, I'm in a very important stage of my life, my senior year of high school. I will do my best to get into my dream college, so I can get a high education, so later I will be a great doctor for those who cannot get proper treatment because of poverty. I'm hoping for the day I can help people as a doctor. That will be the time when I prevail in the game, called *life*.